THE HIGH
MIDDLE AGES,
814–1300

ARCHIBALD R. LEWIS, the editor of this volume in the Sources of Civilization in the West series, is Chairman of the History Department at the University of Massachusetts. He is a specialist in maritime, economic, and institutional history of the Middle Ages and the author of a number of books, including *Naval Power and Trade in the Mediterranean*, A.D. *500–1100* (1950); *The Northern Seas*, A.D. *300–1100* (1958); *The Development of Southern French Catalan Society, 714–1050* (1965); and *Emerging Medieval Europe* (1967).

THE HIGH

MIDDLE AGES,

814–1300

Edited by
Archibald R. Lewis

PRENTICE-HALL, INC.
Englewood Cliffs, New Jersey

A SPECTRUM BOOK

To my wife Elizabeth,
whose help has made possible
this and other books
I have been able to finish
in recent years

FOREWORD

Defining his period as the long stretch of years between the death of Charlemagne in 814 and the end of the thirteenth century, and taking all of western Europe for his base, Professor Lewis has in this volume offered the reader a wide sampling of selections from contemporary writers. After grouping together excerpts from works by men of the court and cloister throughout western Europe in the earlier portion of the period (the Carolingians and the Ottos), he turns in the eleventh century to authors from the individual lands that would become the European nations of the future: France, England, Italy, Germany and the Low Countries, and closes with two sections on Europeans at the fringes of Europe and on Europeans abroad: Scandinavians in Vinland, Frenchmen on their way to Constantinople, and an international expedition to the thriving Moslem port of Lisbon.

No reader who begins this book holding the old-fashioned but still wide-spread view that western Europe was isolated and parochial during these centuries will be able to retain it after the very first of Mr. Lewis's passages, in which we see Louis the Pious in 814, at the center of a continent-wide network of diplomatic communication, in close and regular touch with Scandinavians, Slavs, Byzantines, and Moslems, intervening effectively even to regulate the private conduct of a Pope. The reader's surprise may perhaps grow, when he discovers a German ruler describing the Slavs as "dogs," and thus sowing the wind for the whirlwind he must soon reap; or witnesses the first white men in North America cheerfully slaughtering the first eight out of nine Indians ever seen by Europeans; or listens to a lord of the King of France telling Greek en-

voys to cut out the compliments and get down to cases: so old and
so persistent are the national dislikes and misunderstandings all
too familiar to us in later history and in our own day.

On the other hand, the standard notion that the High Middle
Ages saw continual violence survives unchanged (or even enhanced)
after a careful reading of the book before us. Clerics are admonished
not to continue carrying weapons, and indeed suffer the loss of
their eyes (or in the case of Abelard even more useful members) at
the hands of those who dislike them, while heavy-armed horsemen
clash repeatedly in what seems like perpetual strife, and the air
is full of the whine and buzz of arrows and the twang of bowstrings.
Occasionally we catch a glimpse—in the passages from Otto of
Freising, Villani, or Galbert of Bruges—of people who do not live
wholly by the cross or by the sword: the citizens of Milan, of
Florence, or of Bruges, who are already pushing the world toward
a new line of development, but who are here revealed as even more
turbulently bellicose, if possible, than the fighting men themselves,
while incurring the scorn and distaste of those whose sole occupa-
tions were statecraft and combat. We are of course vouchsafed an
occasional view of gentler pasttimes: that of courtly love, for example, but in this book these are the exceptions that seem to prove
the rule.

No scholar can hope in a small volume like this to convey in all
their variety the rich complexities of a long period of human history, and some might object that here we move about so fast from
time to time and place to place that we see nothing very deeply.
Others might argue that the very variety and sense of movement
transmitted to us here hides from us all the stagnant medieval
backwaters where illiteracy, ignorance, and brutalizing daily labor
characterized human life for century after century. To the first I
would reply that we hope the reader will not stop with this book
but will continue, will read further sources in translation, and then
in the original languages, will study what other scholars have concluded after such research, and will thus round out and deepen his
knowledge of any or all of the regions and periods here introduced.
To the second set of hypothetical critics I would argue that to
catch a student's attention and engage his interest, action is better
than passivity and liveliness than stagnation, always provided that
the editor introduces no distortion. In my belief Mr. Lewis has
succeeded admirably in his endeavor. Even the learned teacher of
medieval history may find here something to astonish him and

broaden his perceptions. How many of you knew before what a desperately wicked woman Leif Eirikson's sister was, or realized why her feet were so cold when she got back into bed in the morning?

Robert Lee Wolff
Archibald Cary Coolidge
Professor of History
Harvard University

CONTENTS

THE HIGH
MIDDLE AGES,
814–1300

Introduction

Between the death of Charlemagne in the first years of the ninth century and the year 1300, Western Europe developed a rich and vital civilization which we call the High Middle Ages. This civilization, which began in faltering fashion during the difficult days of the later Carolingians and the Ottos, had become a richly varied brew by the eleventh, twelfth, and thirteenth centuries. We now find centralized government, economic advance, town life, peasant freedom, chivalry, a rich vernacular romantic literature, new learning in Roman law and rational philosophy, and a distinguished architectural tradition capable of raising intricate fortifications and beautiful Romanesque and Gothic cathedrals.

At the same time this European medieval world had shown the capacity to expand at the expense of its neighbors into Moslem Spain, Syria, and Palestine; into the Byzantine Empire; into tribal areas of the Baltic; and into Celtic Ireland. In short, by 1300 this civilization had become the equal of, or superior to, its sister Chinese, Indian, Moslem, or Byzantine civilizations which had hitherto surpassed it in accomplishments and level of culture.

We are accustomed to viewing this Western European medieval world through the eyes of recent talented historians and to judge it, all too frequently, in the light of their particular prejudices and predilections. A number of phrases they have coined and used spring at once to mind, perhaps unfairly, such as "dark ages," "feudal," "Age of Faith," and the like. But perhaps there is a real advantage to be gained in letting these centuries speak for themselves in the form of contemporary historical, biographical, and other narratives, such as those which are presented here in translation, and which form one of the main bases of our knowledge.

The attentive reader who examines these narrative sources will receive an impression of the civilization of this period in Europe in a direct fashion, without having it filtered through the interpretations which have developed since that time. And even more important, he will find in these writings an unexpected richness and variety which cannot help but interest him.

A number of diverse traditions can be found in the writings of medieval historians and biographers. Initially, down to the thirteenth century, most of them were clerics who wrote in the universal Latin of medieval times, except for a few in Anglo-Saxon England, Scandinavia, and Germany who used their vernacular tongues. The general acquaintance with Latin and the use of it made these medieval writers familiar with a number of Latin classical authors: Juvenal, Sallust, Cicero, Suetonius, Virgil, and Ovid served as stylistic models to an extent surprising to those moderns who think of the cult of antique humanism as the special hallmark of the Renaissance.

But these medieval writers also could and did draw on Christian traditions, especially on the Bible, on St. Augustine's *Confessions* and *City of God*, Boethius' *Consolation of Philosophy*, Orosius' *Seven Books of History Against the Pagans*, Isidore of Seville, and those saints' lives which had emerged as a standard literary form as early as Merovingian times, several centuries before we begin our selections. Nor were special native legendary and historical traditions ignored, such as those of Celtic lands or those which were to form the basis of Norse Sagas and Anglo-Saxon tribal histories.

Finally, of course, these writings reflect the current world in which the authors lived, the wars, the disasters, the triumphs; the trials and the tribulations, individual and collective, of their civilization. It is in that particular combination of the current world about which they were writing with Latin, Christian, Celtic, and Germanic elements that one finds the clue to the varied nature of their presentation.

In noting both the language used and the historical and biographical traditions which animate the authors of this age, one still needs to understand clearly the milieu in which most of this writing took place. Two centers prove to be the most important ones—the court on the one hand, the cloister on the other.

Writing that seems essentially the product of the court may in the early period be seen in that anonymous early biography of Louis the Pious (Selection 1), and in those of Nithard, Asser, and Liudprand of Cremona (Selections 2, 3, and 5). André the Chaplain (Selection 8), Louis IX (Selection 9), John of Salisbury (Selection 14), Otto of Freising (Selection 15), Gerald of Wales (Selection 22), or Odo of Deuil, (Selection 23) all reflect the court, the center of political life, at a later period. These authors wrote out of their special knowledge of the "high politics" and wars with which they had come into contact, just as Thucydides and Polybius did in the ancient world and Arthur Schlesinger, Jr., does today.

But one must also remember the important role played by the

cloister and cathedral in the development of historical and biographical narratives. Charlemagne, in the course of his reign, ordered all abbeys within his empire to keep chronicles—a practice which spread to Spain and the British Isles, and continued to grow unabated in later centuries. By the eleventh century some abbeys, especially those patronized by royalty, and some cathedrals, too, had begun to produce annals and chronicles which were really true histories, semiofficial in character, like those of Reichenau in Germany, St. Albans in England, or Saint Denis in France. The passages written by Ordericus Vitalis (Selection 6), Henry of Huntingdon (Selection 10), Peter of Blois (Selection 11), Matthew of Westminster (Selection 12), the Chronicler of Bury St. Edmunds (Selection 13), Helmhold (Selection 18), or those three annalists who tell us of Richard the Lionhearted's return from the Crusades (Selection 25) are cases in point. Or we might add those biographies and autobiographies which were written by monastics in a cloistered environment like Odo of Cluny's *Life of Saint Gerald of Aurillac* (Selection 4), Peter Abélard's *History of His Misfortunes* (Selection 7) or Bonaventura's *Life of Saint Francis* (Selection 16). Sometimes the official or semiofficial character of these writings is clearly noted, as in the case of the Chronicle of Bury St. Edmunds.

Finally we have included here a few selections of writings which cannot be classified as belonging to either court or cloister. Our two passages from the Sagas (Selections 20 and 21) are the product of a peculiar and highly evolved oral tradition which came to flower in Iceland during the twelfth and thirteenth centuries, if not earlier. Similarly different are the two examples we have of town chronicles; that of Galbert of Bruges (Selection 19) and of Giovanni Villani (Selection 17). They are harbingers of a great town chronicle tradition that later on was to produce Malinstoke of the Netherlands and Macchiavelli of Florence.

When we read these narratives and others like them we make another discovery—how dangerous it is to think of these years as a time in which the average man was mainly concerned with other-worldly considerations. A Bonaventura or an Ordericus Vitalis may, at times, strike an other-worldly note, but though most of these authors were clerics, it is interesting to note how knowingly they can write of war; witness Asser, Ordericus Vitalis himself, Henry of Huntingdon, Matthew of Westminister, Otto of Freising, Helmhold, Gerald of Wales, and Odo of Deuil. In tone churchmen seem to be the most secular-minded, as we can see when we observe the romantic attitudes of Abélard and André the Chaplain or note the way in which Liudprand of Cremona or Peter of Blois view the current scene. On the other hand both Nithard and St. Louis, who were laymen, seem more Christian in their essential interests. To classify these centuries, then, as other-worldly, as an Age of Faith, is simply impossible—judging from these narratives. Medieval man, like modern man, had many moods and myriad interests, some of them secular, some religious.

Similarly we need to dispose of the idea that the medieval world was essentially an illiterate one. The authors presented here obviously wrote for a wide audience that could read and that included by the twelfth century, if not earlier, most nobles of both sexes and the majority of the burgesses of the towns, and perhaps some others. The legend of the illiterate Middle Ages is one that dies hard and is still perpetuated by historians who should know better. Though nothing like mass education existed during these years—despite Charlemagne's hopes in this direction—it seems probable that as large a percentage of the population knew how to read and write as did during the height of the Roman Empire.

Finally, our writers show that these centuries, like our own, were filled with violence and war. Life was varied and colorful, but also dangerous. The warlike hero and villain fill the pages of this book, whether it be the valiant Alfred the Great, an aged William the Conqueror going on his last campaign, a Simon de Montfort in arms defying his liege lord, the crafty murderers of Charles the Good of Flanders, a King Olaf Tryggvason fighting his last battle, a Strongbow conquering Ireland, Florentines rioting in their city streets, or a sister of Leif Ericson plotting the murder of her neighbors in the Vinland settlement. Even a Saint Francis has early dreams of martial glory, and behind the conventional outlines of the typical saint we see in Gerald of Aurillac a well-trained Carolingian warrior. This age of the High Middle Ages, then, saw the growth of a society which was more able to admire peace and Christian concord than to achieve them. Varied in tradition, often secular and sophisticated in their point of view, and worldly in spirit, these narratives show us an era remote from our age in time but similar to it in practice.

Part One

THE AGE OF THE
CAROLINGIANS AND THE
OTTOS

1. Anonymous Biographer: Louis the Pious Takes Over the Empire

This selection, from a life of Louis the Pious by an anonymous author, shows us the young emperor taking over control of the Carolingian realm immediately following the death of his father Charlemagne. The writer, who was probably a younger contemporary of Louis, seems to have been well informed concerning the events of the latter's reign, probably because he had a position at court. He shows us Louis reacting to the scandalous way in which his unmarried sisters had long conducted themselves at Aix-la-Chapelle, his father's capitol. We see him attempting to stabilize his frontiers with the Danes, Slavs, Byzantines, Italians, and Moslems of Spain, while reorganizing the imperial administration and carving out subkingdoms for his sons within the empire. We find him concerned with the revitalization and reform of the Church in a way somewhat different from his father's. And in the revolt of his nephew, Bernard, who was viceroy of Italy, we glimpse the first symptoms of weakness which was to bring about a little later, a decline in imperial power at home and abroad. [From *Son of Charlemagne*, trans. Allen Cabaniss (Syracuse University Press, 1961), pp. 54–66. Copyright © 1961 by Syracuse University Press. Reprinted with the omission of footnotes by permission of the publisher.]

When Charles of holy memory had died, Rampo was sent to Louis by the attendants at the funeral, by the children and magnates of the palace, that he might be informed of the death and that

5

he might in no way delay his coming. As Louis was approaching the city of Orléans,[1] Theodulf, bishop of the see and very learned in all matters, was apprised beforehand. Hurriedly dispatching a reporter to the emperor, Theodulf was eager to discover whether to stand ready as Louis entered the city or to meet him by some route before he entered. Upon consideration Louis discerned the reason and forthwith commanded him to come out to him. Thereafter Louis received sorrowful messengers one after another. After the fifth day he directed his steps from that place and hastened his journey with as many people as perplexity of the time allowed. For Wala, possessor of the highest rank with Emperor Charles, was greatly feared: it was thought that he might plot something sinister against the new emperor. Wala nevertheless came to Louis with all speed and, according to the custom of the Franks, submitted with humble acquiescence, commending himself to the new emperor's will. When he had come to do homage, other Frankish magnates vied in imitation, earnestly and in droves, to meet Louis. Finally he reached Heristal with a favorable journey, and on the thirteenth day after he had removed from Aquitaine[2] he happily placed his foot in the palace of Aachen.[3]

Although by nature very mild he had made up his mind long ago about the activities of his sisters in his father's dwelling (by which blemish alone his father's house was being undermined). Wishing to be rid of that inconvenience and at the same time being on guard lest what had once happened through Odilo and Hiltrud revive a scandal, he sent for Wala and Warnarius as well as for Lantbert and Ingobert. At Aachen they were to look cautiously into such things lest more should happen and also to observe carefully certain ones who by excesssive debauchery and arrogant pride were guilty of *lèse-majesté* at the emperor's entrance. For although some of them had asked for pardon as suppliants while his journey was in progress, they were nonetheless guilty. At the same time he hoped that people who did not come out to meet him might await his arrival there without fear. But without the knowledge of Wala, Ingobert, and Louis's nephew Lantbert, just appointed, Count

---

[1] [Orléans was one of the most important cities of the Carolingian Empire—ED.]

[2] [Louis had been King of Aquitaine before he succeeded his father, Charlemagne, as Emperor—ED.]

[3] [Aachen is another name for Aix-la-Chapelle, the Carolingian imperial capital—ED.]

Warnarius ordered Hodoin, who was already liable to the crime mentioned, to be arrested and exposed to the royal judgment. The latter, forewarned, suspected a plot, for remorse was stinging bitterly. Because he refused to obey, although deserving to be tried, he brought destruction upon Warnarius. For coming as Warnarius had commanded, he killed him and made Lantbert a cripple for a long time with an injury of the leg. He himself, however, was pierced by a sword and slain. When these things had been announced to the emperor, the death of his friend dissuaded his mind from mercy to such a degree that a certain Tullius, who seemed almost worthy of the king's pardon or clemency, was punished by loss of his eyes.

Coming then to the palace of Aix,[4] the emperor was received with great applause by his relatives and many thousands of Franks, and was for the second time proclaimed emperor. Having disposed of these matters, he expressed thanks to those who had been thoughtful of his father's burial and brought the solace of appropriate condolence to kinsmen consumed with bitter grief. What was lacking in the funeral obsequies of his father, he quickly supplied. When his father's will had been read, nothing remained of his father's goods to be distributed according to Louis's discretion, for nothing had been left intestate. What Charles had thought should be apportioned to the metropolitan churches, he had divided by indicating the names, of which there were twenty-one. What was fit for royal equipment he had left to a later time. He had also decreed what should, according to Christian custom, be bequeathed to sons and sons' sons and daughters, to royal servants both male and female, and to the poor folk in common. As Lord Louis the emperor read what was written, he fulfilled all those things, dutifully performing the task.

When these affairs had been completed, the emperor gave sentence that the entire female company (which was very large) be excluded from the palace, except the very few whom he considered fit for the royal service. Each of his sisters withdrew to her own lands which she had received from her father. Although they did not deserve of the emperor such treatment as they got, they yielded to his commands.

Afterwards, respecting the embassies destined for his father but coming to him, the emperor received them with earnestness and listened to them. He tendered them banquets, then sent them away

4 [Or Aachen—ED.]

dowered with expensive gifts. Of them the chief one was from the Emperor Michael of Constantinople,[5] to whom Lord Charles had dispatched as his emissaries Amalarius, bishop of Trèves, and Peter, abbot of Nonantola, to confirm peace. On their return they brought with them emissaries from the aforesaid Michael, Christopher the first swordsman, and Gregory, a deacon, who were accredited to Charles to make reply about all the things which had been written. When the emperor dismissed them, he sent with them his own emissaries to Leo, Michael's successor, Nortbert, bishop of Reggio, and Richoin, count of Poitiers, desiring an alliance and a renewal of old friendship and also a confirmation of the agreement.

In the same year he held a general assembly at Aachen. Throughout all parts of his realm he sent loyal and trusted men, firmly attached to just law and clothed with his authority, to correct evil things and to mete out fitting justice to all with equal balance. Bernard, his nephew and for a long time king of Italy, summoned to his presence and obediently complying, Louis allowed to go back to his own kingdom dowered with ample gifts. Grimoald, prince of the Beneventans, did not come in person but sent his ambassadors. Him he constrained by contract and oaths to contribute every year to the public treasury seven thousand *solidi* of gold.

In the same year he sent his two sons Lothair and Pepin to Bavaria and Aquitaine respectively, but the third, Louis, still in the years of boyhood, he kept with him. At the same time also Heriold, to whom the entire kingdom of the Danes was supposed to belong and who had been driven from that kingdom by the sons of Godefrid, took asylum with Emperor Louis and according to the custom of the Franks entrusted himself to his hands. Having received him, the king ordered him to go to Saxony and there conceal himself for a time until he could bring him help to recover his princedom.

At that time imperial clemency restored to the Saxons and Frisians their ancestral heritage, which because of treachery they had legally lost under his father. Some attributed this act to generosity, others to lack of foresight, on the grounds that since these people were accustomed to native savagery, they ought to be bridled with such reins that they could not dash unrestrained into shameless treason. The emperor, however, supposing that they would be bound to

[5] [There had been friction between the Byzantine emperors and Charlemagne over the latter's assumption of an imperial Roman title. Louis was trying to establish better relations at this time with the new Byzantine emperor—Ed.]

him the more closely to the degree in which he showered kindness upon them, was not deceived in his hope. For afterwards he held the same people as always most devoted to him.

When this year completed its course, it was reported to the emperor that some powerful Romans had entered into a vicious conspiracy against Leo the Apostolic.[6] This apostolic man had adjudged them to be taken away and tried by deadly torture, the law of the Romans being in harmony with that. When the emperor heard these things he was reluctant to believe that punishment had been imposed so severely by the chief priest of the world. He therefore sent King Bernard of Italy thither to investigate what truth or falsity rumor had spread in this matter and to report to him through Gerold. King Bernard then entered Rome and through the aforesaid emissary reported what had been observed. But soon followed the emissaries of Leo the Apostolic, Bishop John of Selva Candida, Theodore the *nomenclator,* and Duke Sergius. They excused Leo the Apostolic for the alleged offenses.

Thereafter the emperor ordered the Saxon and Obotrite counts, formerly subject to Lord Charles, to give aid to Heriold in reclaiming his own realm, Baldricus being sent as legate for this purpose. When these counts had crossed the river Eider, they came down into the land of the Northmen to the place called Sinlendi. Although the sons of Godefrid were abundantly supplied with troops and two hundred ships, they did not want to approach and engage in battle. There was consequently a mutual withdrawal, everything which the counts could destroy being set afire and forty hostages being taken by them. With this achievement they returned to the emperor at a place called Paderborn, where all the people had gathered for a general assembly.

To Paderborn also came all the princes and nobles of the eastern Slavs. Abulat, king of the Saracens, sought from the emperor a three-year truce, which was at first granted but later rejected as worthless. War with the Saracens was thereupon resumed.[7] Bishop Nortbert and Count Richoin came back from Constantinople and brought favorable proposals of treaty between the Greeks and the Franks. At the same season, when Leo the Apostolic was already burdened with adversities, the Romans attempted to steal all the farms which they call "estates" and which had been recently established by the apostolic man, as well as those things which they alleged were robbed of them contrary to law, since no judge had rendered de-

[6] ["The Apostolic" means the Pope—ED.]
[7] [This refers to Emirs of Moslem Spain, not the Caliphs of Baghdad—ED.]

cision. Through Winigis, duke of Spoleto, King Bernard withstood their undertaking and dispatched to the emperor a courier who knew about these events.

After the emperor had passed the harsh winter in sound health and peaceful success and when the favorable mildness of summertime [816] was coming on, those who are called eastern Franks and the counts of the Saxon nation were dispatched by him against the Slavic Sorbs who were reported to have revolted against his domination. Christ granting it, the efforts of these Slavs were suppressed very quickly and easily. But the nearest of the Basques, who dwell in places close to the ridge of the Pyrenees, deserted us at the same time in accordance with their innate fickleness. The cause of the rebellion was the emperor's removal of their Count Sigiwin from chieftaincy over them. The purpose of that action had been to chastise their perverse behavior which he deemed almost intolerable. They were tamed to such a degree by two campaigns that too late they repented of their endeavors and with great eagerness sought to capitulate.

In the midst of these events the falling asleep of Lord Leo, bishop of Rome, which occurred on the eighth day before the Kalends of June in the twenty-first year of his episcopate, was announced to the emperor, as well as the accession of the deacon Stephen to his position. The latter lost no time in coming to the Lord Emperor after his consecration. For two months had scarcely elapsed before he hurried with urgent speed to meet Louis. He sent ahead an embassy to satisfy the emperor about his succession. Anticipating his approach, the emperor ordered his nephew Bernard to accompany him. He also directed others to be sent to conduct him with due honor as he drew nearer. Louis decided to receive his arrival at Rheims and ordered Hildebald, archchaplain of the sacred palace, Theodulf, bishop of Orléans, John of Arles, and a host of other ministers of the church, clad in priestly fillets, to meet him. Lastly the emperor walked in state from the thousand-monk cloister of the holy confessor Remigius and received the vicar of blessed Peter in a most honorable manner; he assisted him in dismounting from his horse and supported him with his own hand as he was entering the church, various ecclesiastical ranks marching in front singing *Te Deum laudamus*. This hymn finished, the clergy of Rome acclaimed the emperor with the due *Laudes*, which the Apostolic Lord completed with a collect.

Afterwards there was a session within the sanctuary of the house. When the reasons for his coming had been rehearsed and the consecrated bread and wine had been shared, the Apostolic Lord remained there while the emperor returned to the city. On the morrow the Lord Emperor called upon the Apostolic Lord, tendered him a sumptuous banquet, and honored him with extensive gifts. In like manner on the third day, the Lord Emperor was invited by the Apostolic Lord and was dowered with many different favors. On the next day, which was the Lord's Day, the emperor was crowned with the imperial diadem and signed with a blessing amid the festivities of Mass. All these things at length completed, the Apostolic Lord returned to Rome, having obtained everything that he had asked. The emperor then retired to Compiègne and there received and heard the emissaries of Abd ar Rahman, son of King Abulat. After twenty or more days there he traveled to Aachen to spend the winter.

The emperor had discreetly bidden the emissaries of the king of the Saracens to precede him as he went thither. When they arrived, they waited almost three months. But since his delay had already wearied them, they went away with the emperor's consent. While he was still in that palace he received a man named Nicephorus, who came as an emissary of Leo, the emperor of Constantinople. There was also a delegation from the regions of the Dalmatians, Romans, and Slavs to continue friendship and alliance. But since neither these nor Chadalo, prefect of the regions, were prompt, and since these things could not be adjusted without them, Albigarius was sent to Dalmatia with Chadalo, chieftain of the regions, to conclude and arrange peace. In the same year, when the sons of Godefrid, formerly king of the Northmen, had been pressed by Heriold, they sent legates to seek peace from the emperor. The legation was repudiated by him as unworthy and feigned, and aid was given instead to Heriold against them. On the Nones of February that year, at the second hour of the night, the moon failed. An unnatural cluster of comets appeared in the sign of Sagittarius. Pope Stephen closed his last day in the third month after he had returned to Rome from Frankland. Paschal came to the Roman pontifical throne in his stead. After the solemn consecration was performed, he sent deputies to the emperor with an explanatory letter and extensive favors, intimating that not by his own effort or desire, but by popular choice and acclamation, he had fallen, rather than leaped, into this dignity. The leader of the deputation was the *nomenclator* Theodore, who returned after the business was transacted and the requests granted, namely, the confirmation of an alliance of friendship according to the custom of their predecessors.

Later in the same year, the period of Lent being almost over, on the fifth feria of the last week (the day on which the memorial of the Lord's Supper is celebrated) and after all things had been performed which the solemnity of so high a day required, it came to pass that, when the emperor sought to withdraw from the church to his royal residence, the lower parts of the wooden colonnade through which he had to go, weakened by decay and age and rotten with continual moisture, cracked and collapsed under the feet of the emperor and his counts. Great terror struck the entire palace with the noise of the crash, everyone fearing that the impact of that fall might have crushed the emperor. But he was protected from the immediate crisis by God to Whom he was a beloved son. For although twenty or more counts fell to the ground with him and met with various mishaps, he incurred no more regrettable damage than a hurt on his stomach where the hilt of his sword hit him and a very small skin-scratch on the lobe of his ear. His leg was also struck near the groin by the same wood, but aid was brought to him very quickly. Summoning skillful physicians, he was restored to his former health in a very short time. Twenty days later indeed he went hunting at Nijmegen.

When that sport was completed the emperor held a general assembly at Aachen where he vigorously declared how much ardor for divine worship he bore in the depth of his heart. The bishops and the noblest clergy of holy church being assembled, he caused the compilation and publication of a book embodying a standard for the canonical life, in which is contained the perfection of that entire order, as one upon reflection acknowledges. In it Louis even ordered to be mentioned the sum, the total amount, of food and drink and of all necessities, so that everyone who served Christ in this order, men as well as nuns, being distracted by no needs, might with unhindered service remember to represent all men before the Lord. This book he distributed throughout all the cities and monasteries of canonical order in his domain by the hands of wise men, who were to cause it to be copied in all the aforesaid places and who were to obtain the cost due and assessed to be paid. This afforded the church a great occasion for rejoicing and constituted for the most pious emperor a deathless memorial of due praise. Likewise the emperor, beloved of God, confirmed Benedict as abbot and appointed with him monks of resolute life to come and go through all monasteries and to entrust everywhere to men and nuns alike a uniform and unalterable manner of living according to the *Rule* of Saint Benedict.

The most pious emperor also, deeming that servants of Christ ought not be obliged to human servitude, but observing that the greed of many men misused the ministry of the church for their own profit, decreed that whosoever of servile status, recommended by learning and honesty of character, was to be admitted to the ministry of the altar, be first manumitted by the particular lords, whether secular or ecclesiastical, and only then be invested with the ranks of the altar. Desiring moreover that each church have its own revenues lest through want divine services be neglected, he inserted in the aforesaid injunction an order that for each church one homestead be assigned with lawful compensation, with both male and female servants. This was the sacred emperor's exercise, this his daily pastime, this his sport, seeing that the state might shine more illustriously in holy teaching and work, and that he might advance higher who in emulation of Christ humbles himself as a poor man in like humility. For it was finally decreed at that time that girdles adorned with golden belts and jeweled daggers be laid aside by bishops and clerics and that fine clothes and spurs on the ankles be abandoned. It was reckoned monstrous if a representative of the church's household should aspire to the accouterments of worldly glory.

The Enemy of mankind did not endure this body and worthy devotion of the emperor to God, but pursued him everywhere and declared war against him in all the ranks of the church. He also undertook to oppose Louis, as the latter attacked him, with an abundance of forces and through his members to harass Christ's brave warrior with what power and craft he could command. After these matters had been arranged properly, the emperor later in the same diet desired his firstborn son, Lothair, to be recognized and designated as co-emperor, and sent his other two sons, Pepin and Louis, to Aquitaine and Bavaria[8] respectively, so that the people might know whose authority to obey. But there was immediately reported to him the defection of the Obotrites who had joined in friendship with the sons of Godefrid and who were harassing Saxony beyond the Elbe. With God's favor the emperor, directing adequate forces against them, checked their movements. Thereafter he entered the forest of the Vosges to hunt. The hunt there was completed after the manner of the Franks, and Louis returned to spend the winter at Aachen.

It was announced that his nephew, Bernard, in whose behalf he had been Charles's chief adviser in making him king of Italy, had been maddened by the counsels of evil men to such a degree that he

[8] [As kings—ED.]

deserted him, that all the cities of the realm and the princes of Italy had conspired at this pretense, and that all the passes by which one has access to Italy they had closed with barriers and guard-posts. When Louis had ascertained this through messengers who informed him, especially Bishop Rathaldus and Suppo, he went as far as Châlon with a great number of troops, forces having been procured from both Gaul and Germany. But when Bernard observed that he himself was unequal in strength and unsuited for the things undertaken (many of his troops were daily falling away from him since matters had become desperate), he came to the emperor and laying down his arms prostrated himself at the emperor's feet, acknowledging that he had acted falsely. His magnates followed his example and also submitted to Louis's power and judgment, laying aside their arms. The questioning of the nobles betrayed how and why they had begun the rebellion, for what purpose they had sought to effect the things thus begun, and whom they alleged to have been their accomplices. The authors of this plot were Eggideo, chief of the royal friends; Reginherius, formerly a count of the emperor's palace and a son of Count Meginherius; also Reginhardus, provost of the royal chamber. A great many clerics and laymen were implicated in the crime, among whom the stormy tempest involved some bishops, Anselm of Milan, Wulfold of Cremona, and Theodulf of Orléans.

2. Nithard: The Wars of Louis' Sons

Nithard, who wrote this account of the wars of the sons of Louis the Pious, after the latter's death, was a well-educated layman, a cousin of Louis' heirs and therefore conversant with the high politics and jealousies that motivated their quarrels. This excerpt from his work tells of the alliance which Charles the Bald and Louis the German developed which resulted in the defeat of their elder brother, Lothaire, and the eventual partition of the Carolingian Empire. The careful reader will note that it reflects a view that God decides the victor in a political and military conflict almost as if it were a trial by combat. One also gets a rare view of those martial exercises used by Carolingian rulers and their upper class as a training for cavalry campaigns. And, last of all, Nithard has managed to produce here the first examples we have of a genuine French dialect or a German dialect in the oaths taken by the two Carolingian monarchs and their followers when they met at Strassbourg to cement their political alliance. [From *Historiarum Libri* by Nithard, ed. Ph. Lauer (Paris: Librarie Ancienne Honore Champion, 1930), Bk. III, Chaps. 5–7, pp. 100–114. Translated by Archbald R. Lewis for this volume by permission of the publisher.]

On the fourteenth of February, 841, Louis and Charles met in that city once called Argentaria, but which is now generally referred to as Strassbourg, and swore, Louis in the Romance or French tongue, Charles in the German one, the oaths which are recorded below. But before swearing such oaths they made suitable speeches to the assembled people, one speaking in German and the other in French, with Louis, the elder, speaking first in these terms.

"You know how many ways Lothaire has vexed us by pursuing us, my brother and me, and attempting to wipe us off the face of the earth. Since neither kinship, nor religious scruples, nor any other thing could keep peace between us, forced by necessity and believing in the justice of our cause, we submitted ourselves to the judgment of Almighty God, trusting in his verdict as concerns our rights. As you know, the result has been that through God's mercy we have won a victory over Lothaire, who, having been vanquished, has fled elsewhere with his followers. But since that time, guided by fraternal affection and filled with compassion for Christian folk, we have not wished to pursue him or vex him further and have only asked—that at least in the future as in time past he treat each of us as we deserve to be treated.

"Despite this fact, refusing to accept God's judgment, he has not desisted from pursuing my brother present here and myself with armed force, and has again brought desolation to our people by burning, pillaging, and massacre. That is why, forced by necessity, we have met here and have decided to swear oaths to each other in your presence to end any kind of doubt as to our determination and brotherly affection.

"We are not doing so in any spirit of base gain for ourselves, but only so that if, with your aid, God gives us victory, we can be assured of an outcome beneficial to us all. If it should happen, and God grant it not be so, that I violate the oath sworn to my brother, I free each of you from all allegiance you owe me according to the oaths you have previously sworn to me."

And after Charles had repeated the same declarations in the French tongue, Louis, being the elder, swore to observe them as follows in French:

"For the love of God and all Christian folk and our common salvation, from today henceforward, insofar as God gives me the power to do so, I will give to my brother Charles assistance and everything else which one brother in fairness owes another and on condition that he do the same with me. And I shall knowingly have no dealings with Lothaire which can have the effect of damaging the interests of my brother Charles."

When Louis had finished Charles repeated the same oath in the German tongue as follows:

"For the love of God and for the salvation of all Christian folk and our own from this day henceforward, insofar as God gives me the power to do so, I shall aid my brother, as one ought rightly to aid one's brother, on condition that he do the same for me. And I will not knowingly enter into any engagements with Lothaire which can have the effect of damaging his interests."

Then each party took an oath in its own tongue which went as follows, [the French-speaking group first]

"If Louis observes the oath which he is swearing to his brother Charles, and if my Lord Charles does not keep his and if neither I nor any others about him can sway him, we will not give him any assistance against Louis." [1]

Then the German-speaking group swore as follows:

" If Charles keeps the oath which he has sworn to his brother Louis and Louis breaks the oath which he has sworn and neither I nor any one else can sway him, we will not give him any assistance against Charles." [2]

When this had been done Louis proceeded along the Rhine towards Worms by way of Spire and Charles along the Vosges by way of Wissembourg.

The summer, during which the battle mentioned above took place, proved to be a very cold one and all the harvests were very late, but autumn and winter followed their normal course. On the very day that the aforementioned brothers and their magnates con-

[1] Si Lodhuuigs sagrament que son fradre Karlo jurat conservat et Karlus, meos sendra, de suo parte non l'ostanit, si io returnar non l'int pois, ne io ne neuls cui eo returnar int pois, in nulla aiudha contra Lodhuuig nun li iu er.

[2] Oba Karl then eid then er sinemo brouodher Ludhuuige gesuor geleistit, indi Ludhuuig, min herro, then er imo guesuor forbrihchit, ob ih inan es iruuenden ne mag, noh ih thero nohhein, then ih es iruunden mag, uuidhar Karle imo ce follusti ne uuirdhit.

cluded their agreements, a hard freeze took place and snow fell in abundance. A comet appeared in December, January, and February during the above meeting and which, rising from the midst of the constellation of Pisces, disappeared, once the parley was concluded, between the constellation of Arcturus and that which some call Lyra and others Andromeda. After these remarks concerning the weather and the courses of the stars, let us again take up the thread of our narrative.

When Louis and Charles arrived at Worms they chose messengers whom they sent to their brother Lothair and to Saxony and decided to await their return and that of Carloman (Louis' son) between Worms and Mainz. At this point it seems not out of place for me to report certain details concerning the personal characteristics of these kings and how they got on with one another. Both of them were of middle height, handsome and skillful in all active pursuits, both were brave, generous, wise, and eloquent, and the sacred and respectful good feelings which reigned between the two brothers surpassed even these noble qualities. They almost always ate together and shared liberally what each had of value. They dealt with their common and private interests with the same generosity and each only asked the other for what he thought would be useful to him.

Often too they joined in sportive exercises in the following manner. They would assemble their followers in a place suitable for such an event, and the whole crowd would take places opposite one another. First the Saxons, the Gascons, the Austrasians, and the Bretons in equal numbers would pursue one another. Then one group of them would turn around and, by taking flight, protected by their armor, would pretend to escape their comrades; then, reversing roles, they in their turn, would pursue those from whom they had fled in the first instance. And finally the kings, on horseback, accompanied by their retinues, would ride into the midst of the melée brandishing their lances and charging sometimes certain groups who were fleeing and sometimes others. And this was a spectacle worth seeing because of the numerous groups of nobles who took part in it, and the fine spirit that reigned throughout the affair. No one, for instance, received any injury among the multitude of diverse peoples who took part and none did anyone any harm, as is frequently the case all too often, among people less numerous who know each other very well.

So things continued until Carloman arrived in Mainz to join his father with a strong force of Bavarians and Alemanni, and Badon, who had been sent to Saxony, returned with the news that the Saxons had rejected overtures made to them by Lothaire and had agreed voluntarily to do what Louis and Charles asked them to do. Despite all this, Lothaire absolutely refused to receive the envoys sent to him, a fact which irritated Louis and Charles and their armed forces and which caused them to decide to move against him.

Therefore on the seventeenth of March, 842, they began to march north into Lothaire's lands, Charles by way of the Vosges, Louis by way of Bingen along the Rhine Valley, and Carloman by way of Enriche, and after some nine hours of the next day they arrived at Coblenz. They went at once to pray and hear mass at the Church of Saint Castor and then the kings and their armed forces boarded boats to cross the Moselle. When Ottaker, the Archbishop of Mainz, Count Halton, Harold, and all those that Lothaire had posted there to keep them from crossing the river saw them arrive, they were seized with fear and fled from the river bank. Lothaire also, when he learned at Sinzig that his brothers had crossed the Moselle, hastened to flee his capitol and his kingdom (of Lorraine) and, abandoning all others, took refuge with several partisans who decided to accompany him in the region of the Rhone river.

Thus, with the end of this second campaign which Lothaire fought, our third book ends.

3. Asser: Alfred the Great

Alfred the Great has always seemed to most historians to have been England's ideal medieval king—indeed the only one in her long history called the Great—and these excerpts from his biography by Asser show why this is so. Bishop Asser, who lived during the late ninth century and first came in contact with Alfred in 884, obviously knew him rather intimately. And, though his writing presents an idealized formal view of this monarch, with special embellishments added to it by later authors, like the story of the burnt cakes, what emerges is the portrait of an authentic royal hero. Alfred's principal task, it seems clear, was that of defending his realm against heathen Danish invaders. And in doing so neither he nor his predecessors had much time for peaceful pursuits, as the story of his difficulty in learning to read makes clear. Nevertheless, the king who emerged from this ordeal was so vitally interested in justice, religious life, and scholarship that he laid the foundations of the more peaceful and cultured England of the High Middle Ages. Indeed without Alfred and his accomplishments, shown in part in these passages, the Britain of later times seems almost inconceivable. [From *Life of King Alfred* by Asser, trans. L. C. Jane (London: Chatto and Windus Ltd, 1924), pp. 17–20, 22–23, 29–31, and 42–45. Reprinted by permission of the publisher.]

But, to use nautical similies, we will no longer entrust our ship to the waves and winds, nor will we put out far from land and steer amid so many bloody wars and chronicles of years. For I think it well that we should return to that which chiefly led me to undertake this work, or in other words, I propose here to relate shortly what little has come to my knowledge concerning the character of my revered Lord Alfred, king of the Anglo-Saxons, in his infancy and in his boyhood.

Now he was greatly cherished above all his brothers by the united and ardent love of his father and mother, and indeed of all people; and he was ever brought up entirely at the royal court. As he passed through his infancy and boyhood he surpassed all his brothers in beauty, and was more pleasing in his appearance, in his speech, and in his manners. From his earliest childhood the noble character of his mind gave him a desire for all things useful in this present life, and, above all, a longing for wisdom; but, alas! the culpable negligence of his relations, and of those who had care of him, allowed him to remain ignorant of letters until his twelfth year, or even to a later age. Albeit, day and night did he listen attentively to the Saxon poems, which he often heard others repeating, and his retentive mind enabled him to remember them.

An ardent hunter, he toiled persistently at every form of that art, and not in vain. For in his skill and success at this pursuit he surpassed all, as in all other gifts of God. And this skill we have ourselves seen on many occasions.

Now it chanced on a certain day that his mother showed to him and to his brothers a book of Saxon poetry, which she had in her hand, and said, "I will give this book to that one among you who shall the most quickly learn it." Then, moved at these words, or rather by the inspiration of God, and being carried away by the beauty of the initial letter in that book, anticipating his brothers who surpassed him in years but not in grace, he answered his mother, and said, "Will you of a truth give that book to one of us? To him who shall soonest understand it and repeat it to you?" And at this she smiled and was pleased, and affirmed it, saying, "I will give it to him." Then forthwith he took the book from her hand and went to his master, and read it; and when he had read it he brought it back to his mother and repeated it to her.

After this he learnt the Daily Course, that is, the services for each hour, and then some psalms and many prayers. These were collected in one book, which, as we have ourselves seen, he constantly carried about with him everywhere in the fold of his cloak, for the sake of prayer amid all the passing events of this present life. But, alas! the art of reading which he most earnestly desired he did not acquire in accordance with his wish, because, as he was wont himself to say, in those days there were no men really skilled in reading in the whole realm of the West Saxons.

With many complaints, and with heartfelt regrets, he used to declare that among all the difficulties and trials of this life this was the greatest. For at the time when he was of an age to learn, and had leisure and ability for it, he had no masters; but when he was older, and indeed to a certain extent had anxious masters and writers, he could not read. For he was occupied day and night without ceasing both with illnesses unknown to all the physicians of that island, and with the cares of the royal office both at home and abroad, and with the assaults of the heathen by land and sea. None the less, amid the difficulties of this life, from his infancy to the present day, he has not in the past faltered in his earnest pursuit of knowledge, nor does he even now cease to long for it, nor, as I think, will he ever do so until the end of his life.

*   *   *

In the year of the Incarnation of the Lord eight hundred and sixty-eight, which was the twentieth year from the birth of King Alfred, the same revered King Alfred, being then the recognised heir to the kingdom, sought and obtained a wife from Mercia. She was of noble birth, being the daughter of the ealdorman of the Gaini, Ethelred, surnamed Mucill. Her mother's name was Eadburh, of the royal stock of the king of the Mercians, and on her we often fixed the very gaze of our own eyes not many years before her death. She was a venerable matron, and for many years, from the death of her husband to the day of her own death, remained a widow in the utmost chastity.

In the same year the aforesaid army of the pagans departed from the Northumbrians and came into Mercia. And it reached Nottingham, which, being interpreted, is in the British tongue Tigguocobauc, but in Latin "speluncarum domus"; and in that year the army wintered in that place. On the arrival of the heathen, Burhred, king of the Mercians, and all the nobles of the same people, forthwith sent messengers to Ethelred, king of the West Saxons, and to Alfred, his brother, making humble petition that they would come to their help, that they might be able to fight with the said army; and they obtained their prayer with ease. So those brothers, not being slack in the performance of their promise, gathered a great army from every side and entered Mercia, and came in company as far as Nottingham, seeking battle. And when the heathen, being safe in the protection of the fortress, would not give battle, and when the Christians could not break down the wall, peace was made between the Mercians and the pagans, and those two brothers, Ethelred and Alfred, returned home.

*   *   *

When these things had thus befallen there, again after fourteen days, King Ethelred and Alfred, his brother, united their forces to fight against the heathen, and came to Basing. When battle had been joined on both sides, and had for a long while continued, the pagans gained the victory and held the place of slaughter. And after the battle was ended another pagan army came from the lands across the sea and joined itself to the host.

And in the same year, after Easter, the said King Ethelred, after that he had for five years, amid many tribulations, ruled the kingdom with ability and honour and in good fame, went the way of all flesh. And he was buried in the monastery of Wimborne, and awaits the Advent of the Lord and the first resurrection with the just.

In that year this same Alfred, who up to that time, while his brothers lived, had been the recognised heir to the throne, by a grant of divine providence and with the full assent of all the inhabitants of that land, at once upon the death of his brother received the rule of the whole realm. And even while that same brother yet lived, had he wished to receive it, he could most easily have obtained the government, with the assent of all men, since of a truth both in wisdom and in all good qualities he surpassed all his brothers, and moreover because he was very warlike and was victorious in almost every battle. He began to reign, then, as it were against his will, inasmuch as he did not think that it was within his power, trusting in the aid of God alone, ever to withstand such great fierceness of the heathen, since, while his brothers yet lived, he had suffered many and manifold trials.

Then, when he had reigned one full month, with a few men and an army of which the number was very unequal to the task, he contended with the whole host of the pagans on a hill named Wilton, lying on the southern bank of the river Wylye, wherefrom all that district takes its name. And when for no small part of the day the battle had been contested on both sides and in every part of the field fiercely and strenuously, the pagans with their own eyes perceived the full extent of their danger, and no longer bearing the onslaught of their enemies, they turned and fled. But, alas! they deceived our men into rash pursuit, and again entering into the battle, they secured the victory and held the place of slaughter.

Nor need this cause wonder to any one, since the number of the Christians in that battle was small. For by the eight battles with the pagans in that one year, in the which one of the kings of the pagans, and nine chieftains, besides soldiers innumerable, had fallen, the Saxons were in general almost utterly worn out. And this takes no account of the countless attacks by day and by night which the oft-mentioned Alfred, and all the chief men of that people, with their followers, and very many of the king's thegns also, made upon the heathen, with zest and without wearying. And how many thousands of the pagan host were slain in these constant attacks, that is, who fell over and above those who fell in the eight battles already mentioned, is known to none save to God.

In this year also the Saxons made an agreement with the pagans on this condition that they should depart from them. This also the pagans did.

*   *   *

And when the next day was now dawning the king moved his camp thence and came to the place which is called Aecglea, and there camped for one night. And at dawn on the following day he set his standards in motion and came to the place called Edington. And he fought fiercely against the whole host of the pagans, forming his shield-wall closely, and striving long and boldly. And at the last, by God's help, he gained the victory, and with great slaughter overthrew the pagans, and smiting the fugitives, pursued them to the fort. And all things, men and horses and beasts, that he found without the fort he took, and the men he slew forthwith.

Then he boldly pitched his camp, with all his host, before the gates of the pagan [Danish built] fortress. And when he had abode there fourteen days the pagans were overcome by hunger and cold and fear, and at the last despaired. Then they sought peace on these terms that the king should receive from them hostages, as many as he would, and that he should give no hostage to them; and never, indeed, had they made peace with any one on the like terms. And when he had heard their embassy the king was moved with pity and received from them chosen hostages, as many as he desired; and after they had been received the pagans also swore that they would straightway depart from his realm. Moreover Guthrum, their king, in addition promised that he would accept Christianity and would receive baptism at the hand of King Alfred.

And he and his men performed all these things as they had promised. For after seven weeks Guthrum, the king of the pagans [Danes] with thirty of the most chosen men of his army, came to King Alfred at a place called Aller, near to Athelney, and King Alfred received him as his son by adoption and raised him from the holy font of baptism. And his chrism-loosing was on the eighth day, at the royal residence which is called Wedmore. And after that he was baptised he remained twelve nights with the king, and to him and to all his men the king gave freely many and excellent articles of goldsmiths' work.

In the year of the Incarnation of the Lord eight hundred and seventy-nine, which was the twenty-eighth year from the birth of King Alfred, the same pagan army, departing from Chippenham, as they had promised, went to Cirencester, which is called in the British tongue Cairceri, and which is in the south part of the land of the Hwiccas. There it remained one year.

In the same year an army of the pagans sailed from the lands across the sea and came into the river Thames, and joined the former army. Yet it passed the winter in a place near to the river Thames, Fulham by name.

And in this year there was an eclipse of the sun, between nones and vespers, but nearer to nones.

In the year of the Incarnation of the Lord eight hundred and eighty, which was the twenty-ninth year from the birth of King Alfred, the oft-mentioned army of the pagans left Cirencester and went into the land of the East Angles, and meting out that region began to dwell therein.

In the same year the army of the pagans which had passed the winter at Fulham left the island of Britain, and sailed again across the sea, and came to East Francia, and remained one year in the place that is called Ghent.

In the year of the Incarnation of the Lord eight hundred and eighty-one, which was the thirtieth year from the birth of King Alfred, the same army went farther into the land of the Franks, and the Franks fought against it, and when the battle was ended the pagans found horses and became horsemen.

In the year of the Incarnation of the Lord eight hundred and eighty-two, which was the thirty-first year from the birth of King Alfred, the same army drew its ships up the river which is called Meuse [in Belgium] and went much farther into Francia, and there wintered for one year.

And in the same year Alfred, king of the Anglo-Saxons, fought a battle with ships in the sea against the pagan ships, and he took two of them and slew all who were in them. And the two commanders of two other ships, with all their comrades, being much wearied with the battle and with their wounds, laid down their arms, and, with bended knee and suppliant prayers, gave themselves up to the king.

4. Odo of Cluny: Count Gerald of Aurillac, a Late Ninth-Century French Magnate

One often finds it difficult to visualize just how a powerful noble behaved during those years when the Carolingian Empire was decaying and a more feudalized France was slowly beginning to take form north of the Midi. Fortunately for us we have a picture of such a figure in this biography of St. Gerald of Aurillac written about 930 by Odo, a great tenth-century abbot of Cluny, who was almost Gerald's contemporary. No doubt Gerald was a better Christian than many of his noble contemporaries who left France a shambles as they pursued their family feuds. But, as we see him here, he ran his allodial estates—lands owned outright without any feudal obligations—dispensed justice on his own and managed his household, his retainers, and his officials without reference to any outside authority whatsoever. We view him as he travels to Rome on pilgrimages, takes care of the poor peasants who work his land, and fights against rapacious neighbors and other forces of local disorder. In short, in this account the realities of aristocratic control of the tenth-century French countryside are revealed to us clearly and succinctly. [From *St. Odo of Cluny*, trans. and ed. Dom Gerard Sitwell, O.S.B. (London: Sheed and Ward Ltd, 1958), pp. 94–101 and 109–18. Copyright © 1858 by Sheed and Ward Ltd. Reprinted with omission of footnotes by permission of the publisher.]

The man of God, Gerald, took his origin from that part of Gaul which was called by the ancients *Celtica*, in the territory which marches with that of Auvergne and Cahors and Albi, in the town or village of Aurillac. His father was Gerald, his mother Adaltruda. He was so illustrious by the nobility of his birth, that among the families of Gaul his lineage is outstanding both for its possessions and the excellence of its life. For it is said that his parents held modesty and religion as a sort of hereditary dowry. Two witnesses among his ancestors are themselves sufficient to prove the point: namely St. Caesarius, the Bishop of Arles, and the holy Abbot Aredius. . . . And indeed the great quantity of estates endowed with serfs, lying in various places, which came to Gerald by right of succession, testifies to the extent of their riches. But in him the beauty of mind which he inherited from his parents shone forth much augmented. With what grace were his parents endowed, who merited to beget so excellent an offspring!

*   *   *

When he had been born, . . . and weaned, and had come to that age in which the character of children may usually be discerned, a certain pleasing quality began to show itself in him, by which those who looked closely conjectured of what virtue the future man should be. For at an early age, as we often see, children through the incitements of their corrupt nature are accustomed to be angry and envious, and to wish to be revenged, or to attempt other things of this sort. But in the child Gerald a certain sweetness and modesty of mind, which especially graces youth, adorned his childish acts. By the grace of divine providence he applied himself to the study of letters, but by the will of his parents only to the extent of going through his psalter; after that he was instructed in the worldly exercises customary for the sons of the nobility; to ride to hounds, become an archer, learn to fly falcons and hawks in the proper manner. But lest given to useless pursuits the time suitable for learning letters should pass without profit the divine will ordained that he should be a long time sick, though with such a sickness that he should be withdrawn from worldly pursuits but not hindered in his application to learning. And for a long time he was so covered with small pimples that it was not thought that he could be cured. For this reason his father and mother decided that he should be put more closely to the study of letters, so that if he should prove unsuited for worldly pursuits, he might be fitted for the ecclesiastical state. So it came about that he not only learnt the chant, but also learnt something of grammar. And this was afterwards of much use to him, since, perfected by that exercise, his wits were sharpened for whatever he might wish to apply them to. He had a lively and discerning mind, and was not slow to learn anything to which he set himself.

While he was growing up his bodily strength consumed the harmful humours of his body. So agile was he that he could vault over the backs of horses with ease. And because, endowed with bodily strength as he was, he became very active, it was demanded of him that he accustom himself to military service. But the sweetness of the Scriptures, to the study of which he was greatly attracted, held his mind in pledge, so that, although he excelled in military exercises, nevertheless it was the charm of letters which attracted him. In the former by a voluntary sloth he was a little slow, in the latter he was assiduous. I believe now he began to perceive that according to the testimony of Scripture, wisdom is better than strength, and that nothing is more precious. And because it is easily perceived by those that love it, wisdom took possession of his mind to reveal itself to him and to be the sweet expression of his thought. Nothing was able to hinder Gerald from hastening to the love of learning. So it came about that he learnt almost the whole series of the Scriptures and surpassed many clerical smatterers in his knowledge of it.

After the death of his parents, when he attained full power over his property, Gerald was not puffed up, as youths often are who boast of their grown-up mastery, nor did he change the modesty which was springing up in his heart. His power of ruling increased, but the humble mind did not grow haughty. He was compelled to be occupied in administering and watching over things which, as I have said, came to him by hereditary right, and to leave that peace of heart, which he had to some extent tasted, to take up the weariness of earthly business. He could scarcely bear to leave the inner solitude of his heart, and he returned to it as soon as he could. . . .

He admitted these gnawing cares unwillingly for the sake of the complaints of those who had recourse to him. For his dependents pleaded querulously saying: "Why should a great man suffer violence from persons of low degree who lay waste his property?", adding that, when these discovered that he did not wish to take vengeance they devoured the more greedily that which was rightfully his. It would be more holy and honest that he should recognize the right of armed force, that he should unsheathe the sword against his enemies, that he should restrain the boldness of the violent; it would be better that the bold should be suppressed by force of arms than that the undefended districts should be unjustly oppressed by them. When Gerald heard this he was moved, not by the attack made on him but by reason, to have mercy and to give help. Committing himself entirely to the will of God and the divine mercy, he sought only how he might visit the fatherless and widows and hold himself unspotted from this world, according to the precept of the Apostle.

He therefore exerted himself to repress the insolence of the violent, taking care in the first place to promise peace and most easy reconciliation to his enemies. And he did this by taking care, that either he should overcome evil by good, or if his enemies would not come to terms, he should have in God's eyes the greater right on his side. And sometimes indeed he soothed them and reduced them to peace. When insatiable malice poured scorn on peaceful men, showing severity of heart, he broke the teeth of the wicked, that, according to the saying of Job, he might snatch the prey from their jaws. He was not incited by the desire for revenge, as in the case with many, or led on by love of praise from the multitude, but by love of the poor, who were not able to protect themselves. He acted in this way lest, if he became sluggish through an indolent patience, he should seem to have neglected the precept to care for the poor. He ordered the poor man to be saved and the needy to be freed from the hand of the sinner. Rightly, therefore, he did not allow the sinner to prevail. But sometimes when the unavoidable necessity of fighting lay on him, he commanded his men in imperious tones, to fight with the backs of their swords and with their spears reversed. This would have been ridiculous to the enemy if Gerald, strengthened by divine power, had not been invincible to them. And it would have seemed useless to his own men, if they had not learnt by experience that Gerald, who was carried away by his piety in the very moment of battle, had not always been invincible. When therefore they saw that he triumphed by a new kind of fighting which was mingled with piety, they changed their scorn to admiration, and sure of victory they readily fulfilled his commands. For it was a thing unheard of that he or the soldiers who fought under him were not victorious. But this also is certain, that he himself never wounded anybody, nor was wounded by anyone. . . . Let no one be worried because a just man sometimes made use of fighting, which seems incompatible with religion. No one who has judged his cause impartially will be able to show that the glory of Gerald is clouded by this. . . . Gerald did not fight invading the property of others, but defending his own, or rather his people's rights, knowing that the rhinoceros, that is, any powerful man, is to be bound with a thong that he may break the clods of the valley, that is, the oppressors of the lowly.

*　　　　　*　　　　　*

At meal times great respect was paid to him. Chattering or buffoonery had no place at his table but the talk was of necessary or virtuous subjects, or indeed of religious ones. At all times of the year he dined once in the day, unless perhaps in the summer when he supped off something simple and uncooked. At his table there was always reading for some time to begin with; but for the sake of the seculars present he used to suspend the reading at intervals, and ask the clerics what had been said in it—those whom he knew to be able to reply. He had noble clerics at his board to whom he eagerly imparted both good behaviour and learning. To the adolescent he showed himself more austere, saying that that age was very dangerous, when a youth put off the voice and appearance of his mother and began to assume the voice and appearance of his father; and one who took care to guard himself at that time, he said, might easily overcome thenceforth the movements of the flesh. When those whom he asked about the reading requested that he should rather speak himself, he used to offer them not a pompous dissertation, but a speech of learning and simplicity. When those were present who would bring forward something facetious or jocular, as used to happen, he restrained them not with biting indignation, but as though by joking also. But he never allowed idle talk to be protracted in his presence. . . . At the end of the meal the reader always repeated what had been read. So Gerald spent the greater part of meal times speaking with God, or with God speaking to him through the reading. . . .

He always wore woollen or linen clothes of the old fashion, and not in that which the sons of Belial, who are without restraint, have devised and follow in our day. His were so made that they neither suggested pompous affectation, nor drew attention by plebeian rusticity. He took care not to adorn himself more than usual with silken or precious garments either because of the occurrence of any feast or the presence of any dignitary, and he would not change or renew his sword-belt for twenty years if it would last so long. What shall I say of the belts, the twisted cinctures, the buckles, the decorated medallions for horses, when he not only forbade himself to wear gold, but even to possess it. . . .

The poor and the wronged always had free access to him, nor did they need to bring the slightest gift to recommend their cause. For the more fully anyone brought his necessity to his notice, the more closely did he attend to his need. And now his goodness was heard of not only in neighbouring, but also in distant regions. And because everyone knew his kindness to all, many found the solution of their difficulties in him. Nor did he disdain either personally or through his officials to interest himself in the affairs of the poor, and, as occasion offered, to give help. For often when he knew that there was fierce strife between litigants, on the day on which the cause was to be heard he had Mass said for them, and implored the divine assistance for those whom, humanly speaking, he could not help. Nor did he allow any lord to take benefices from a vassal because he was angry with him. But when the case was brought forward, partly by entreaty, partly by command, he allayed the exasperation. You might think the vigour of his justice severe in this one thing alone, that whenever a poor man was brought before a more powerful man, he was at hand to uphold the weaker, in such a way that the stronger was overcome without being hurt. For the rest, truly hungering after justice, he insisted on its being carried out not only among his own people but even among strangers. . . .

Robbers had taken possession of a certain wood, and plundered and murdered both passers-by and those who lived in the vicinity. Gerald, hearing of this, immediately gave orders for them to be captured. It happened, however, that a certain countryman was driven by fear to join them. But the soldiers who captured them, fearing that Gerald would either release them, or blame them for showing him the prisoners unpunished, forthwith put out the eyes of all of them. And so it came about that this countryman was blinded. Later he went into the district of Toulouse, and a long time afterwards, when Gerald heard that he had not been a companion of the robbers, he was very grieved, and asked if he was still alive, and where he had gone. Having learnt that he had gone to the province of Toulouse, he sent him, so they say, a hundred shillings, ordering the messenger to ask pardon for him from the man.

How he mercifully consoled the afflicted, and often spared the guilty, may be seen from an example. His neighbours had afflicted a certain priest with increasing quarrels, to the point that they put out his eyes. The count consoled the man greatly by his words, urging him to be patient. But lest the consolation of words should seem meagre, he handed over to him a certain church in his jurisdiction by formal deed. After a little time one of those who had done violence to the priest was taken by the officers and shut up in prison, and this was forthwith announced to the count as something over which he would rejoice. And he in haste, as though with the desire of punishing the man, went to the prison. But other cases arose which it was necessary to deal with on the next day, and so he ordered the accused to be kept till then. In the evening when the officers had gone home, he secretly ordered the jailer to refresh the man with food and drink. And because he had no shoes he allowed shoes to be given to him and permitted him to escape. On the next day when those who were attending the court came to the count, he ordered the accused to be brought forth, and some men whom the jailer had prepared to act on his behalf announced trembling that the accused had escaped. Gerald, wishing to conceal the truth, made as though to threaten the jailer, but soon he said, "It is well, for the priest has now forgiven the injury done to him."

So, two men in chains were presented to him accused of a great crime. The accusers insisted that he should order them forthwith to be hanged. He dissembled, because he did not wish to free them openly. For he so conducted himself in any good work, that the goodness did not appear too much. Looking therefore at the accusers, "If", he said, "they ought to die, as you say, let us first give them a meal in the customary manner." Then he ordered food and drink to be brought to them, and ordered them to be unbound so that they might eat. When they had eaten he gave them his knife saying, "Go yourselves and bring the osier with which you must be hanged." Not far away was a wood which grew up thickly with saplings. Going into this as though looking for osiers and gradually penetrating further they suddenly disappeared, and so escaped the moment of death. Those who were present, understanding that it was with his consent, did not dare to search for them among the bushes. He punished either with fines or branding the accused who were, as far as could be judged from their appearance, confirmed in evil. But those who had done wrong not through seasoned malice but inadvertently, he set free uncondemned. It was unheard of, nevertheless, that anyone was punished by death or maiming in his presence.

Of the many things he did let me recall a few particular examples which will suffice to show certain acts of goodness which are known to me. For this reason, too, I insert certain small facts through which his great zeal may be illustrated, as for example the following. Once while he was going along by the road, a countrywoman was guiding the plough in an adjoining field. He asked her why she was doing a man's work. She replied that her husband had been long ill, that the time of sowing was passing, she was alone and had no one to help her. Having pity on her calamities, he ordered as many coins to be given her as there were days of sowing left over, so that on each day she might hire a labourer and she herself cease from doing the work of a man. Nature flees from everything artificial, as Ambrose says, and its author, God, abhors what is unnatural. This is a small thing in itself, but the attitude of a just man in agreement with the laws of nature makes it become great.

On another occasion as he was going along the road a peasant was reaping chick-peas nearby. Some of his retinue, who were in front, took some of it and began to eat it. When he saw this, spurring his horse, he came at full speed to the man, asking if his followers had taken the chick-pea. "I gave it to them freely," he said. "May God reward you!" Gerald replied.

An incident of the same kind is that which occurred when his servants were preparing a meal under the shade of some cherry trees. He bought for silver from a peasant who was claiming them some branches which were hanging down loaded with ripe fruit, which the servants had broken off before he came. . . .

To his vassals he was so kind and peaceable that it was a matter of wonder to those who saw it. And they frequently complained that he was soft and timid, because he permitted himself to be injured by persons of low degree as though he had no authority. Nor was he easily or lightly annoyed, as lords generally are, by his critics. On one occasion he met a number of peasants who had left their holdings, and were moving into another province. When he had recognized them and inquired where they were going with their household goods, they replied that they had been wronged by him when he had given them their holdings. The soldiers who were accompanying him urged that he should order them to be beaten and made to go back to the holdings from which they had come. But he was unwilling. . . . He therefore permitted them to go where they thought they would be better off, and give them permission to live there. Not without shame I recently heard some idle tattle that he used not to remit the debts of a man who was in pledge to him, but that is quite false, as those bear witness who often saw him remit not only the interest but also the capital.

His tenants and clerics, who loved him dearly as a father, often brought him bundles of wax, which he with many thanks accepted as great gifts. And he did not allow any of this wax to be burnt for his own use, but he ordered it all to be burnt in lights before the altar or the relics of the saints, which he had carried about with him. The servants of his bedchamber, when it happened that there was no wax ready for his service, prepared birch bark or pinewood torches. But how could one who was so careful that private people should not use the gifts which had been freely given him, exact strict payment from those who had pledged themselves? Rather, he often remitted to the debtors more than they owed to him by right. . . .

Once on his way back from Rome as he was going past Pavia he made his camp not far from the city. The Venetians and many others hearing of this immediately went out to him, for he was quite the most celebrated traveller on that road, and was known to all as a religious and generous man. When therefore the traders, as their manner is, were going about among the tents and enquiring if anybody wanted to buy anything, some of the more considerable among them came to Gerald's tent and asked the retainers whether the lord count (for so they all called him) would order some cloaks or spices. He himself called them and said, "I bought what I wanted in Rome; but I should like you to tell me whether I bought wisely." Then he ordered the cloaks that he had got to be brought out. Now, one of them was very valuable, and a Venetian looking at it, asked what he had given for it. When he had learnt the price, "Indeed," he said, "if it was at Constantinople it would be worth even more." When the count heard this he was horrified, as though in dread of a great crime. Afterwards, therefore, when he met some Roman pilgrims whom he knew, he gave them as many shillings as the Venetian had said the cloak was worth more than the price he had given for it, telling them where they could find the seller of the cloak. Truly, while men are accustomed to have compunction for other kinds of sin, and to consider amendment, rarely or never will you see anyone except Gerald who regrets having transgressed in a sin of this kind. But indeed he knew that God is offended by all sin, and he did not wish to offend even in the smallest things Him whom he loved with his whole heart. . . .

5. Liudprand of Cremona: Otto I and Popes John XII and Leo VIII

Bishop Liudprand of Cremona (920–72), who wrote this spirited account of Otto I's relationship with Popes John XII and Leo VIII, has given us one of the few sources we possess that informs us of events in Italy during the mid-tenth century. He also writes with a vividness and a spicy prejudice that many have found fascinating. Furthermore, though one must, in fairness, discount some of the picture he paints for us, he does reveal a papacy which had decayed and become corrupted since Carolingian times. It was now the creature of a quarrelsome and dissolute Roman nobility, until Otto I made an effort to bring reform and order to it. One also senses the gap which seems already to exist between a rather sophisticated Italian world and the simpler and more moralistic milieu of Germany beyond the Alps. Thus, in a curious way, Otto I's difficulties with John XII already point the way towards later quarrels between papacy and empire which were to mark medieval history during the late eleventh, twelfth, and thirteenth centuries. [From *Liber de Rebus Gestis Ottonis,* in *The Works of Liudprand of Cremona,* trans. F. A. Wright (London: George Routledge and Sons, Ltd., 1930), pp. 224–32. Reprinted with omission of footnotes by permission of Routledge & Kegan Paul Ltd.]

When he had heard this, as the Romans could not understand his native Saxon tongue, the emperor [Otto] bade Liudprand bishop of Cremona to deliver the following speech in the Latin language to all the Romans.[1] Accordingly he got up and began thus: "It often happens, and we know it by experience that men set in high positions are besmirched by the foul tongue of envy: the good displease the bad, even as the bad displease the good. For this reason we still regard as doubtful the charge against the pope which

[1] [Otto I was at Rome where he was attempting to reorganize and reform the papacy during these years as part of his imperial responsibilities—ED.]

the cardinal deacon Benedict read out and communicated to you, and we are uncertain whether it originated from zeal for righteousness or from impious envy. Therefore, unworthy as I am, by the authority of the position that has been granted me I call upon you all by the Lord God, whom no one, even if he wishes, can deceive, and by his holy mother the pure virgin Mary, and by the most precious body of the chief of the apostles, in whose church this is now being read, cast no foul words against the lord pope nor accuse him of anything that he has not really done and that has not been witnessed by men on whom we can rely." Thereupon the bishops, the priests, the deacons, the rest of the clergy, and the whole Roman people cried out as one man:—"If Pope John has not committed all the shameful crimes that the deacon Benedict read out to us and done things even worse and more disgusting than those, may the most blessed Peter, whose verdict closes the gates of heaven against the unworthy and opens them for the righteous, never free us from the chains of our sins: may we be held fast in the bonds of anathema and at the last day be set on the left hand with those who said to the Lord God: 'Depart from us, we would have no knowledge of thy ways.' If you do not give us credence, at least you ought to believe the army of our lord the emperor, against whom the pope advanced five days ago, equipped with sword, shield, helmet and cuirass. It was only the intervening waters of the Tiber that saved him from being taken prisoner in that garb." Then the holy emperor said:—"There are as many witnesses to that as there are fighting men in our army." So the holy synod pronounced: "If it please the holy emperor, let a letter be sent to the lord pope, that he come here and purge himself from all these charges." Thereupon a letter was sent to him as follows:

"To the supreme pontiff and universal pope lord John, Otto, august emperor by the grace of God, together with the archbishops and bishops of Liguria, Tuscany, Saxony and France, sends greeting in the name of the Lord. When we came to Rome in God's service and inquired of your sons, the Roman bishops, cardinal priests and deacons, and the whole body of the people besides, concerning your absence, and asked them what was the reason that you were unwilling to see us, the defenders of your church and your person, they brought out such foul and filthy tales about you that we should be ashamed of them, even if they were told about actors. That your highness may not remain in complete ignorance we set down some of them briefly here; for though we would fain give them all seriatim, one day is not enough. Know then that you are charged, not by a few men but by all the clergy and laity alike, of homicide, perjury, sacrilege and of the sin of unchastity with your own kinswoman and with two sisters. They tell me too something that makes me shudder, that you have drunk wine for love of the devil, and that in dice you have asked the help of Jupiter, Venus and the other demons. Therefore we earnestly beg your paternal highness not to refuse under any pretence to come to Rome and clear yourself of all these charges. If perchance you fear the violence of a rash multitude, we declare under oath that no action is contemplated contrary to the sanction of the holy canons."

After reading this letter, the pope sent the following reply: "Bishop John, servant of God's servants, to all the bishops. We hear say that you wish to make another pope. If you do, I excommunicate you by Almighty God, and you have no power, to ordain no one or celebrate mass."

When this answer was read in the holy synod, the following clergy, who had been absent at the previous meeting, were present: from Lorraine, Henry Archbishop of Trèves; from Aemilia and Liguria, Wido of Modena, Gezo of Tortona, Sigulf of Piacenza. The synod returned the following reply to the lord Pope:—"To the supreme pontiff and universal pope lord John, Otto, august emperor by the grace of God, and the holy synod assembled at Rome in God's service, send greeting in the Lord's name. At our last meeting of the sixth of November we sent you a letter containing the charges made against you by your accusers and their reasons for bringing them. In the same letter we asked your highness to come to Rome, as is only just, and to clear yourself from these allegations. We have now received your answer, which is not at all of a kind suited to the character of this occasion but is more in accordance with the folly of rank indifference. There could be no reasonable excuse for not coming to the synod. But messengers from your highness ought certainly to have put in an appearance here, and assured us that you could not attend the holy synod owing to illness or some such insuperable difficulty. There is furthermore a sentence in your letter more fitting for a stupid boy than a bishop. You excommunicated us all if we appointed another bishop to the see of Rome, and yet gave us power to celebrate the mass and ordain clerical functionaries. You said:—'You have no power to ordain no one.' We always thought, or rather believed, that two negatives make an affirmative, if your authority did not weaken the verdict of the authors of old. However, let us reply, not to your words, but to your meaning. If you do not refuse to come to the

synod and to clear yourself of these charges, we certainly are prepared to bow to your authority. But if—which Heaven forbid!—
under any pretence you refrain from coming and defending yourself against a capital charge, especially when there is nothing to
stop you, neither a sea voyage, nor bodily sickness, nor a long
journey, then we shall disregard your excommunication, and rather
turn it upon yourself, as we have justly the power to do. Judas, who
betrayed, or rather who sold, Our Lord Jesus Christ, with the other
disciples received the power of binding and loosing from their
Master in these words:—'Verily I say unto you, Whatsoever ye shall
bind on earth shall be bound in heaven: and whatsoever ye shall
loose on earth shall be loosed in heaven.' As long as Judas was a
good man with his fellow disciples, he had the power to bind and
loose. But when he became a murderer for greed and wished to
destroy all men's lives, whom then could he loose that was bound
or bind that was loosed save himself, whom he hanged in the
accursed noose?" This letter was written on the twenty-second day
of November and sent by the hand of the cardinal priest Adrian
and the cardinal deacon Benedict.

When these latter arrived at Tivoli, they could not find the
pope: he had gone off into the country with bow and arrows, and
no one could tell them where he was. Not being able to find him
they returned with the letter to Rome and the holy synod met for
the third time. On this occasion the emperor said: "We have waited
for the pope's appearance, that we might complain of his conduct
towards us in his presence: but since we are now assured that he
will not attend, we beg you earnestly to listen to an account of his
treacherous behaviour. We hereby inform you, archbishops, bishops,
priests, deacons, clerics, counts, judges and people, that Pope John
being hard pressed by Berengar and Adalbert, our revolted subjects,
sent messengers to us in Saxony, asking us for the love of God to
come to Italy and free him and the church of St. Peter from their
jaws. We need not tell you how much we did for him with God's
assistance: you see it to-day for yourselves. But when by my help
he was rescued from their hands and restored to his proper place,
forgetful of the oath of loyalty which he swore to me on the body
of St. Peter, he got Adalbert to come to Rome, defended him against
me, stirred up tumults, and before my soldiers' eyes appeared as
leader in the campaign equipped with helmet and cuirass. Let the
holy synod now declare its decision." Thereupon the Roman pon-
tiffs and the other clergy and all the people replied: "A mischief for
which there is no precedent must be cauterized by methods equally

novel. If the pope's moral corruption only hurt himself and not others, we should have to bear with him as best we could. But how many chaste youths by his example have become unchaste? How many worthy men by association with him have become reprobates? We therefore ask your imperial majesty that this monster, whom no virtue redeems from vice, shall be driven from the holy Roman church, and another be appointed in his place, who by the example of his goodly conversation may prove himself both ruler and benefactor, living rightly himself and setting us an example of like conduct." Then the emperor said: "I agree with what you say; nothing will please me more than for you to find such a man and to give him control of this holy universal see."

At that all cried with one voice:—"We elect as our shepherd Leo, the venerable chief notary of the holy Roman church, a man of proved worth deserving of the highest sacerdotal rank. He shall be the supreme and universal pope of the holy Roman church, and we hereby reprobate the apostate John because of his vicious life." The whole assembly repeated these words three times, and then with the emperor's consent escorted the aforesaid Leo to the Lateran Palace amid acclamations, and later at the due season in the church of St. Peter elevated him to the supreme priesthood by holy consecration and took the oath of loyalty towards him.

When this had been arranged the most holy emperor, hoping that he could stay at Rome with a few men and not wishing the Roman people to be burdened with a great army, gave many of his soldiers leave to return home. John, the so-called pope, hearing of this and knowing how easily the Romans could be bribed, sent messengers to the city, promising the people all the wealth of St. Peter and the churches, if they would fall upon the pious emperor and the lord pope Leo and impiously murder them. Why make a long tale? The Romans encouraged, or rather ensnared by the fewness of the emperor's troops and animated by the promised reward, at once sounded their trumpets and rushed in hot haste upon the emperor to kill him. He met them on the bridge over the Tiber, which the Romans had barricaded with waggons. His gallant warriors, well trained in battle with fearless hearts and fearless swords, leaped forward among the foe, like hawks falling on a flock of birds, and drove them off in panic without resistance. No hiding place, neither basket nor hollow tree trunk nor filthy sewer, could protect them in their flight. Down they fell, and as usually happens with such gallant heroes, most of their wounds were in the back. Who of the Romans then would have escaped from the massacre, had not the holy emperor yielded to the pity, which they did not deserve, and called off his men still thirsting for the enemies' blood.

After they were all vanquished and the survivors had given hostages, the venerable pope Leo fell at the emperor's feet and begged him to give the hostages back and rely on the people's loyalty. At the request of the venerable pope Leo the holy emperor gave back the hostages, although he knew that the Romans would soon start the trouble I am about to relate. He also commended the pope to the Romans' loyalty, a lamb entrusted to wolves; and leaving Rome hastened towards Camerino and Spoleto where he had heard that Adalbert was to be found.

Meanwhile the women, with whom the so-called pope John was accustomed to carry on his voluptuous sports, being many in numbers and noble in rank, stirred up the Romans to overthrow Leo, whom God and they themselves had chosen as supreme and universal pope, and bring John back again into Rome. This they did; but by the mercy of God the venerable pope Leo escaped from their clutches and with a few attendants made his way to the protection of the most pious emperor Otto.

The holy emperor was bitterly grieved at this insult, and to avenge the expulsion of the lord pope Leo and the foul injuries done by the deposed John to the cardinal deacon John and the notary Azo, one of whom had his right hand cut off, and the other his tongue, two fingers and his nose, he got his army together again and prepared to return to Rome. But before the holy emperor's forces were all assembled, the Lord decreed that every age should know how justly Pope John had been repudiated by his bishops and all the people, and how unjustly afterwards he had been welcomed back. One night when John was disporting himself with some man's wife outside Rome, the devil dealt him such a violent blow on the temples that he died of the injury within a week. Moreover at the prompting of the devil, who had struck the blow, he refused the last sacraments, as I have frequently heard testified by his friends and kinsmen who were at his death bed.

At his death the Romans, forgetful of the oath they had taken to the holy emperor, elected Benedict cardinal deacon as pope, swearing moreover that they would never abandon him but would defend him against the emperor's might. Thereupon the emperor invested the city closely and allowed no one to get out with a whole skin. Siege engines and famine completed the work, and finally in spite of the Romans he got possession of the city again, restored the venerable Leo to his proper place, and bade Benedict the usurper to appear before him.

Accordingly the supreme and universal pope the lord Leo took his seat in the church of the Lateran and with him the most holy emperor Otto, together with the Roman and Italian bishops, the archbishops of Lorraine and Saxony, the bishops, priests, deacons and the whole Roman people whose names will be given later. Before them appeared Benedict, the usurper of the apostolic chair, brought in by the men who had elected him and still wearing the pontifical vestments. To him the cardinal archdeacon Benedict addressed the following charge: "By what authority or by what law, O usurper, are you now wearing this pontifical raiment, seeing that our lord the venerable pope Leo is alive and here present, whom you and we elected to the supreme apostolic office when John had been accused and disowned? Can you deny that you swore to our lord the emperor here present that you and the other Romans would never elect nor ordain a pope without the consent of the emperor and his son King Otto?" Benedict replied:—"Have mercy upon my sin." Then the emperor, revealing by his tears how inclined he was to mercy, asked the synod not to pass hasty judgment upon Benedict. If he wished and could, let him answer the questions and defend his case: if he had neither the wish nor the power but confessed his guilt, then let him for the fear of God have some mercy shown to him. Thereupon Benedict flung himself in haste at the feet of the lord pope Leo and the emperor, and cried out: "I have sinned in usurping the holy Roman see." He then handed over the papal cloak and gave the papal staff which he was holding to pope Leo, who broke it in pieces and showed it to the people. Next the pope bade Benedict to sit down on the ground and took from him his chasuble and stole. Finally he said to all the bishops: "We hereby deprive Benedict, usurper of the holy Roman apostolic chair, of all pontifical and priestly office: but by reason of the clemency of the lord emperor Otto, by whose help we have been restored to our proper place, we allow him to keep the rank of deacon, not at Rome but in exile, which we now adjudge against him."

Part Two

 FRANCE

6. Ordericus Vitalis: The Last Campaign and Death of William the Conqueror

Some scholars have spoken of Ordericus Vitalis (1075–1143), who lived for most of his adult life as a monk in the Norman monastery of St. Evoul, as the best French historian of his age. The following passages from his writings reveal why this is so. They show us the aged and corpulent William the Conqueror as he went on his last campaign in France and died in the Norman duchy where he was born. We also see him attempting to set his affairs in order as he sensed the approach of death, and we get a rather macabre account of his botched burial in Rouen, his ducal capital. Especially interesting is the way in which Ordericus uses such scenes to point a moral as to the vanity of earthly power and possessions, even when they are enjoyed by a powerful and energetic ruler. One senses from all this how close medieval man felt to God and eternity, and how transitory the things of this world were, no matter what station in life one occupied. [From *The Ecclesiastical History of England and Normandy* by Ordericus Vitalis, trans. Thomas Forester (London: Henry G. Bohn, 1854; George Bell and Sons, 1883), II, 398–402 and 417–23.]

The old feuds between the Normans and French being renewed, hostilities again burst forth, and the flames of war occasioned the most serious losses both to the clergy and laity. For Hugh, surnamed Stavel, and Ralph Malvoisin, and other inhabitants of the fortified town of Mantes took up arms against King William, and collecting a large band of freebooters made frequent predatory excursions into Normandy. Crossing in the night, at the head of their troops, the river Eure which divides Normandy from France, they threw themselves unexpectedly on the diocese of Evreux determined on committing the most cruel devastations. The brunt of the inroad fell on the domains of William de Breteuil in the neighbourhood of Paci, and those of Roger de Ivri, from which they drove off herds of cattle, and carried away many prisoners, so that deriding the Normans, they were beyond measure elated at their success. This induced the warlike King William, who was excessively enraged, to lay claim to the whole province of the Vexin, requiring Philip, king of France, to surrender Pontoise, Chaumont, and Mantes, and making terrible threats against his enemies if he was not restored to his lawful rights.

❋　　　　❋　　　　❋

Upon this, William made his appearance suddenly before Mantes, at the head of an army, in the last week of the month of July, and his troops entered the city mixed with the garrison. For the townsmen had stolen out of the place to observe the devastations which Ascelin Goël had made with the Norman troops the day before the king's arrival, by burning the standing corn, and rooting up the vines. The royal army thus rushing in pell-mell with the garrison, passed the gates, and in their fury set fire to the castle, which was burnt, with the churches and houses. It was there that King William, who was very corpulent, fell sick from the excessive heat and his great fatigues, languishing six weeks with severe sufferings. There were some who rejoiced at this calamity, hoping to have free scope for pillage and robbing their neighbours' substance, others, who looked for security in peace, greatly feared the death of their lord, on whom it depended. The king, who during his whole life had followed the advice of wise counsellors, had feared God as became his faithful servant, and had been the unwearied protector of holy mother church, maintained his exalted reputation to the end. His death was worthy of his life. To the very last, through all his illness, his intellect was clear and his conversation lively; repenting of his sins he confessed them to the priests of God, and humbly strove to appease his wrath according to the rites of the Christian church. The bishops, abbots, and men of religion never left him, and were indefatigable in opening to the dying prince the salutary doctrines of eternal life. The noise of Rouen, which is a populous place, becoming insupportable to the sufferer, the king gave orders that he should be conveyed out of the city to the church of St. Gervase, standing on a hill to the west, which his grandfather, Duke Richard, had given to the monastery of Fécamp. There, Gilbert, bishop of Lisieux, and Guntard, abbot of Jumièges, with some others, well skilled in medicine, carefully watched over him, devoting themselves zealously to their master's welfare, both spiritual and temporal.

At length, his disorder continually increasing, and perceiving that inevitable death was becoming imminent, he became anxious about the future, which was veiled from his sight, reflecting on which with deep concern, he was frequently moved to sighs and groans. He summoned to his side his sons William Rufus and Henry, who were in attendance on him with some of his friends, and gave them many wise and prudent directions for the regulation of his states. Robert, his eldest son, had long since entered on a course of repeated quarrels with his father, and had recently taken umbrage in consequence of some new follies, and retired to the court of the king of France.

The wise king hastened to make provision for the future welfare of himself and others, ordering all his treasures to be distributed among the churches, the poor, and the ministers of God. He exactly specified the amount to be given to each, and gave directions to the notaries to reduce it to writing in his own presence. He also contritely sent large donations to the clergy of Mantes, to be applied to the restoration of the churches he had burnt. He gave admonitions to all who were present relative to the maintenance of justice and good faith, keeping the law of God and peace, the privileges of the churches, and observing the rules of the fathers.

*   *   *

At length, on Tuesday, . . . the 9th of September, the king waking just when the sun was beginning to shed his rays on the earth, heard the sound of the great bell of the cathedral of Rouen. On his inquiring what it meant, his attendants replied: "My Lord, the bell is tolling for primes in the church of St. Mary." Then the king, raised his eyes to heaven with deep devotion, and lifting up his hands said: "I commend myself to Mary, the holy mother of God, my heavenly mistress, that by her blessed intercession I may be reconciled to her well-beloved Son, our Lord Jesus Christ." Having said this he instantly expired. The physicians and others who were present, who had watched the king all night while he slept, his repose neither broken by cries or groans, seeing him now expire so suddenly and unexpectedly, were much astonished, and became as men who had lost their wits. Notwithstanding, the wealthiest of them mounted their horses and departed in haste to secure their property. But the inferior attendants, observing that their masters had disappeared, laid hands on the arms, the plate, the robes, the linen, and all the royal furniture, and leaving the corpse almost naked on the floor of the house hastened away.

Observe then, I pray you, my readers, how little trust can be placed in human fidelity. All these servants snatched up what they could of the royal effects, like so many kites, and took to their heels with their booty. Roguery thus came forth from its hiding place the moment the great justiciary was dead, and first exercised its rapacity round the corpse of him who had so long repressed it.

* * *

Meanwhile, the citizens of Rouen having heard the death of their prince, were in the greatest state of alarm; almost all of them lost their reason, as if they had been intoxicated, and were thrown into as much confusion as if the city had been threatened with an assault by a powerful army. Each quitted the place where he received the news, and ran to confer with his wife, or the first friend or acquaintance he met, as to what was to be done. Every one removed, or prepared to remove, his valuables, concealing them with alarm, lest they should be discovered.

At length the religious, both clergy and monks, recovering their courage and the use of their senses, formed a procession; and, arrayed in their sacred vestments, with crosses and censers, went in due order to St. Gervase, where they commended the spirit of the departed king to God, according to the holy rites of the Christian faith. Then William, the archbishop, ordered the body to be conveyed to Caen, and interred there in the abbey of St. Stephen the protomartyr, which the king himself had founded. His brother and other relations had already quitted the place, and all his servants had deserted him, as if he had been a barbarian; so that not one of the king's attendants was found to take care of his corpse. However, Herluin, a country knight, was induced by his natural goodness to undertake the charge of the funeral, for the love of God and the honour of his country. He therefore procured at his own expense persons to embalm and carry the body; and, hiring a hearse, he caused it to be carried to the port on the Seine; and, embarking it on board a vessel, conducted it by water and land to Caen.

Then Gilbert, the lord abbot, with the whole convent of monks, met the hearse in solemn procession, accompanied by a sorrowing multitude of clerks and laymen, offering prayers. But at this moment a sudden calamity filled the minds of all with alarm. For a fire broke out in one of the houses, and, shooting up prodigious volumes of flame, spread through great part of the town of Caen, doing great damage. The crowds, both of clergy and laity, hastened with one accord to extinguish the fire, so that the monks were left alone to finish the service they had begun, and they brought the royal corpse into the abbey church, chanting psalms. . . .

The mass ended, when the coffin was already lowered into the grave, but the corpse was still on the bier, the great Gilbert, bishop of Evreux, ascended the pulpit, and pronounced a long and eloquent discourse on the distinguished character of the deceased prince. He expatiated on William's having extended by his valour the bounds of the Norman dominion, and raised his people to a pitch of greatness surpassing the times of any of his predecessors; and on his having maintained peace and justice in all his states, wisely chastising thieves and robbers with the scourge of the law, while he firmly defended the clergy and monks, and defenceless people, with his meritorious sword. When he had concluded his discourse he addressed himself to the congregation, who were shedding affectionate tears and attested his assertions, and added this supplication: "As in this present life no man can live without sin, I beseech you, for the love of Christ, that you earnestly intercede with Almighty God on behalf of our deceased prince, and that you kindly forgive him, if in aught he has offended against you."

Then Ascelin, son of Arthur, came forward from the crowd, and preferred the following complaint with a loud voice, in the hearing of all: "The land," he said, "on which you stand was the yard belonging to my father's house, which that man for whom you pray, when he was yet only duke of Normandy, took forcible possession of, and in the teeth of all justice, by an exercise of tyrannical power, here founded this abbey. I therefore lay claim to this land, and openly demand its restitution, and in God's name I forbid the body of the spoiler being covered with earth which is my property, and buried in my inheritance." The bishops and other great men, on hearing this, and finding from inquiries among his neighbours that he spoke the truth, drew the man aside, and, instead of offering him any violence, appeased his resentment with gentle words and came to terms with him. For the small space in which the grave was made, they paid him on the spot sixty shillings, and promised him a proportionable price for the rest of the land which he claimed. This agreement they soon afterwards fulfilled, for the good of the soul of the master they dearly loved.

However, when the corpse was lowered into the stone coffin, they were obliged to use some violence in forcing it in, because through the negligence of the masons it had been made too short, so that, as the king was very corpulent, the bowels burst, and an intolerable stench affected the by-standers and the rest of the crowed. The smoke of incense and other aromatics ascended in clouds, but failed to purify the tainted atmosphere. The priests therefore hurried the conclusion of the funeral service and retired as soon as possible, in great alarm, to their respective abodes. . . .

A king once potent, and warlike, and the terror of the numberless inhabitants of many provinces, lay naked on the floor, deserted by those who owed him their birth, and those he had fed and enriched. He needed the money of a stranger for the cost of his funeral, and a coffin and bearers were provided, at the expense of an ordinary person, for him, who till then had been in the enjoyment of enormous wealth. He was carried to the church, amidst flaming houses, by trembling crowds, and a spot of freehold land was wanting for the grave of one whose princely sway had extended over so many cities, and towns, and villages. His corpulent stomach, fattened with so many delicacies, shamefully burst, to give a lesson, both to the prudent and the thoughtless, on what is the end of fleshly glory. Beholding the corruption of that foul corpse, men were taught to strive earnestly, by the rules of a salutary temperance, after better things than the delights of the flesh, which is dust, and must return to dust. . . .

7. Peter Abélard: The History of His Misfortunes

Peter Abélard (1079–1142) was a monumental figure in the revival of learning in Western Europe and one of those who made rational scholastic theology an exciting subject for students who

were attending the growing cathedral schools of the twelfth century. This account of his early days in Paris and elsewhere in
Northern France, though it was written in his old age, is thus of
special interest to us. In it he makes clear—with that special pride
of intellect which he never was able to overcome—what life was
like in the scholarly circles of his youth. He also relates the
poignant story of his love affair with Héloise, who in some ways
was very much his moral superior—a love affair which ended
tragically for all concerned. What seems particularly interesting to
note in Abélard's account is the way in which he shows that France,
and Paris in particular, had by his day developed a special and
critical concern for learning of an intellectual sort—one that still
distinguishes it in these existential days of Sartre and Simone de
Beauvoir. [From *The Story of My Misfortunes: An Autobiography
by Peter Abélard*, trans. Henry Adams Bellows (Glencoe, III.: The
Free Press, 1958), pp. 1–6, 14–22, 29–30. Copyright 1922, © 1958 by
The Free Press of Glencoe. Reprinted by permission of the publisher.]

Know, then, that I am come from a certain town which
was built on the way into lesser Brittany, distant some eight miles, as
I think, eastward from the city of Nantes, and in its own tongue
called Palets. Such is the nature of that country, or, it may be, of
them who dwell there—for in truth they are quick in fancy—that
my mind bent itself easily to the study of letters. Yet more,
I had a father who had won some smattering of letters before he
had girded on the soldier's belt. And so it came about that long
afterwards his love thereof was so strong that he saw to it that each
son of his should be taught in letters even earlier than in the
management of arms. Thus indeed did it come to pass. And because I was his first born, and for that reason the more dear to
him, he sought with double diligence to have me wisely taught.
For my part, the more I went forward in the study of letters, and
ever more easily, the greater became the ardour of my devotion to
them, until in truth I was so enthralled by my passion for learning
that, gladly leaving to my brothers the pomp of glory in arms, the
right of heritage and all the honours that should have been mine
as the eldest born, I fled utterly from the court of Mars that I
might win learning in the bosom of Minerva.[1] And since I found the
armory of logical reasoning more to my liking than the other forms
of philosophy, I exchanged all other weapons for these, and to the
prizes of victory in war I preferred the battle of minds in disputation.

[1] [Abélard means he eschewed a warlike noble career to follow a life of
scholarship—Ed.]

Thenceforth, journeying through many provinces, and debating as I went, going whithersoever I heard that the study of my chosen art flourished, I became such an one as the Peripatetics.[2]

I came at length to Paris, where above all in those days the art of dialectics was most flourishing, and there did I meet William of Champeaux, my teacher, a man most distinguished in his science both by his renown and by his true merit. With him I remained for some time, at first indeed well liked of him; but later I brought him great grief, because I undertook to refute certain of his opinions, not infrequently attacking him in disputation, and now and then in these debates I was adjudged victor. Now this, to those among my fellow students who were ranked foremost, seemed all the more insufferable because of my youth and the brief duration of my studies.

Out of this sprang the beginning of my misfortunes, which have followed me even to the present day; the more widely my fame was spread abroad, the more bitter was the envy that was kindled against me. It was given out that I, presuming on my gifts far beyond the warranty of my youth, was aspiring despite my tender years to the leadership of a school; nay, more, that I was making ready the very place in which I would undertake this task, the place being none other than the castle of Melun, at that time a royal seat. My teacher himself had some foreknowledge of this, and tried to remove my school as far as possible from his own. Working in secret, he sought in every way he could before I left his following to bring to nought the school I had planned and the place I had chosen for it. Since, however, in that very place he had many rivals, and some of them men of influence among the great ones of the land, relying on their aid I won to the fulfillment of my wish; the support of many was secured for me by reason of his own unconcealed envy. From this small inception of my school, my fame in the art of dialectics [philosophy and logic] began to spread abroad, so that little by little the renown, not alone of those who had been my fellow students, but of our very teacher himself, grew dim and was like to die out altogether. Thus it came about that, still more confident in myself, I moved my school as soon as I well might to the castle of Corbeil, which is hard by the city of Paris, for there I knew there would be given more frequent chance for my assaults in our battle of disputation.

No long time thereafter I was smitten with a grievous illness, brought upon me by my immoderate zeal for study. This illness

[2][That is to say, Abélard became one of the logicians of the period—ED.]

forced me to turn homeward to my native province, and thus for some years I was as if cut off from France. And yet, for that very reason, I was sought out all the more eagerly by those whose hearts were troubled by the lore of dialectics. But after a few years had passed, and I was whole again from my sickness, I learned that my teacher, that same William Archdeacon of Paris, had changed his former garb and joined an order of the regular clergy. . . .

To him did I return, for I was eager to learn more of rhetoric from his lips; and in the course of our many arguments on various matters, I compelled him by most potent reasoning first to alter his former opinion on the subject of the universals, and finally to abandon it altogether. Now, the basis of this old concept of his regarding the reality of universal ideas was that the same quality formed the essence alike of the abstract whole and of the individuals which were its parts: in other words, that there could be no essential differences among these individuals, all being alike save for such variety as might grow out of the many accidents of existence. Thereafter, however, he corrected this opinion, no longer maintaining that the same quality was the essence of all things, but that, rather, it manifested itself in them through diverse ways. This problem of universals is ever the most vexed one among logicians, to such a degree, indeed, that ever Porphyry, writing in his "Isagoge" regarding universals,[3] dared not attempt a final pronouncement thereon, saying rather: "This is the deepest of all problems of its kind." Wherefore it followed that when William had first revised and then finally abandoned altogether his views on this one subject, his lecturing sank into a state of negligent reasoning that it could scarce be called lecturing on the science of dialectics at all; it was as if all his science had been bound up in this one question of the nature of universals.

Thus it came about that my teaching won such strength and authority that even those who before had clung most vehemently to my former master, and most bitterly attacked my doctrines, now flocked to my school.

*　　　　*　　　　*

[M]y school was notably increased in size by reason of my lectures on subjects of both these kinds [theology and philosophy], and the

[3] [This was a famous text concerning logic by one of the leading Greek philosophers—ED.]

amount of financial profit as well as glory which it brought me cannot be concealed from you, for the matter was widely talked of. . . . Thus I, who by this time had come to regard myself as the only philosopher remaining in the whole world, and had ceased to fear any further disturbance of my peace, began to loosen the rein on my desires, although hitherto I had always lived in the utmost continence. And the greater progress I made in my lecturing on philosophy or theology, the more I departed alike from the practice of the philosophers and the spirit of the divines in the uncleanness of my life. For it is well known, methinks, that philosophers, and still more than those who have devoted their lives to arousing the love of sacred study, have been strong above all else in the beauty of chastity.

Thus did it come to pass that while I was utterly absorbed in pride and sensuality, divine grace, the cure for both diseases, was forced upon me, even though I, forsooth, would fain have shunned it. First was I punished for my sensuality, and then for my pride. For my sensuality I lost those things whereby I practiced it; for my pride, engendered in me by my knowledge of letters— . . . I knew the humiliation of seeing burned the very book in which I most gloried. And now it is my desire that you should know the stories of these two happenings, understanding them more truly from learning the very facts than from hearing what is spoken of them, and in the order in which they came about. . . .

Now there dwelt in that same city of Paris a certain young girl named Héloïse, the niece of a canon who was called Fulbert. Her uncle's love for her was equalled only by his desire that she should have the best education which he could possibly procure for her. Of no mean beauty, she stood out above all by reason of her abundant knowledge of letters. Now this virtue is rare among women, and for that very reason it doubly graced the maiden, and made her the most worthy of renown in the entire kingdom. It was this young girl whom I, after carefully considering all those qualities which are wont to attract lovers, determined to unite with myself in the bonds of love, and indeed the thing seemed to me very easy to be done. So distinguished was my name, and I possessed such advantages of youth and comeliness, that no matter what woman I might favour with my love, I dreaded rejection of none. Then, too, I believed that I could win the maiden's consent all the more easily by reason of her knowledge of letters and her zeal therefor; so, even if we were parted, we might yet be together in thought with the aid of written messages. Perchance, too, we might be able to write more boldly than we could speak, and thus at all times could we live in joyous intimacy.

Thus, utterly aflame with my passion for this maiden, I sought to discover means whereby I might have daily and familiar speech with her, thereby the more easily to win her consent. For this purpose I persuaded the girl's uncle, with the aid of some of his friends, to take me into his household—for he dwelt hard by my school—in return for the payment of a small sum. My pretext for this was that the care of my own household was a serious handicap to my studies, and likewise burdened me with an expense far greater than I could afford. Now, he was a man keen in avarice, and likewise he was most desirous for his niece that her study of letters should ever go forward, so, for these two reasons, I easily won his consent to the fulfillment of my wish, for he was fairly agape for my money, and at the same time believed that his niece would vastly benefit by my teaching. More even than this, by his own earnest entreaties he fell in with my desires beyond anything I had dared to hope, opening the way for my love; for he entrusted her wholly to my guidance, begging me to give her instruction whensoever I might be free from the duties of my school, no matter whether by day or by night, and to punish her sternly if ever I should find her negligent of her tasks. In all this the man's simplicity was nothing short of astounding to me; I should not have been more smitten with wonder if he had entrusted a tender lamb to the care of a ravenous wolf. When he had thus given her into my charge, not alone to be taught but even to be disciplined, what had he done save to give free scope to my desires, and to offer me every opportunity, even if I had not sought it, to bend her to my will with threats and blows if I failed to do so with caresses? There were, however, two things which particularly served to allay any foul suspicion: his own love for his niece, and my former reputation for continence.

Why should I say more? We were united first in the dwelling that sheltered our love, and then in the hearts that burned with it. Under the pretext of study we spent our hours in the happiness of love, and learning held out to us the secret opportunities that our passion craved. Our speech was more of love than of the books which lay open before us; our kisses far outnumbered our reasoned words. Our hands sought less the book than each other's bosoms; love drew our eyes together far more than the lesson drew them to the pages of our text. In order that there might be no suspicion, there were, indeed, sometimes blows, but love gave them, not anger; they were the marks, not of wrath, but of a tenderness surpassing the most fragrant balm in sweetness. What followed? No degree in love's progress was left untried by our passion, and if love itself could imagine any wonder as yet unknown, we discovered it. And our inexperience of such delights made us all the more ardent in our pursuit of them, so that our thirst for one another was still unquenched.

In measure as this passionate rapture absorbed me more and more, I devoted ever less time to philosophy and to the work of the school. Indeed it became loathsome to me to go to the school or to linger there; the labour, moreover, was very burdensome, since my nights were vigils of love and my days of study. My lecturing became utterly careless and lukewarm; I did nothing because of inspiration, but everything merely as a matter of habit. I had become nothing more than a reciter of my former discoveries, and though I still wrote poems, they dealt with love, not with the secrets of philosophy. Of these songs you yourself well know how some have become widely known and have been sung in many lands, chiefly, methinks, by those who delighted in the things of this world. As for the sorrow, the groans, the lamentations of my students when they perceived the preoccupation, nay, rather the chaos, of my mind, it is hard even to imagine them. . . .

It was not long after this that Héloïse found that she was pregnant, and of this she wrote to me in the utmost exultation, at the same time asking me to consider what had best be done. Accordingly, on a night when her uncle was absent, we carried out the plan we had determined on, and I stole her secretly away from her uncle's house, sending her without delay to my own country. She remained there with my sister until she gave birth to a son, whom she named Astrolabe. Meanwhile her uncle, after his return, was almost mad with grief; only one who had then seen him could rightly guess the burning agony of his sorrow and the bitterness of his shame. What steps to take against me, or what snares to set for me, he did not know. If he should kill me or do me some bodily hurt, he feared greatly lest his dear-loved niece should be made to suffer for it among my kinsfolk. He had no power to seize me and imprison me somewhere against my will, though I make no doubt he would have done so quickly enough had he been able or dared, for I had taken measures to guard against any such attempt.

At length, however, in pity for his boundless grief, and bitterly blaming myself for the suffering which my love had brought upon him through the baseness of the deception I had practiced, I went

to him to entreat his forgiveness, promising to make any amends that
he himself might decree. I pointed out that what had happened
could not seem incredible to any one who had ever felt the power
of love, or who remembered how, from the very beginning of the
human race, women had cast down even the noblest men to utter
ruin. And in order to make amends even beyond his extremest hope,
I offered to marry her whom I had seduced, provided only the thing
could be kept secret, so that I might suffer no loss of reputation
thereby. To this he gladly assented, pledging his own faith and that
of his kindred, and sealing with kisses the pact which I had sought
of him—and all this that he might the more easily betray me.

*   *   *

So after our little son was born, we left him in my sister's care,
and secretly returned to Paris. A few days later, in the early morning, having kept our nocturnal vigil of prayer unknown to all in
a certain church, we were united there in the benediction of wed-
lock, her uncle and a few friends of his and mine being present. We
departed forthwith stealthily and by separate ways, nor thereafter
did we see each other save rarely and in private, thus striving our
utmost to conceal what we had done. But her uncle and those of
his household, seeking solace for their disgrace, began to divulge
the story of our marriage, and thereby to violate the pledge they
had given me on this point. Héloïse, on the contrary, denounced
her own kin and swore that they were speaking the most absolute
lies. Her uncle, aroused to fury thereby, visited her repeatedly with
punishments. No sooner had I learned this than I sent her to a convent of nuns at Argenteuil, not far from Paris, where she herself
had been brought up and educated as a young girl. I had them
make ready for her all the garments of a nun, suitable for the life
of a convent, excepting only the veil, and these I bade her put on.

When her uncle and his kinsmen heard of this, they were con-
vinced that now I had completely played them false and had rid myself forever of Héloïse by forcing her to become a nun. Violently
incensed, they laid a plot against me, and one night, while I, all
unsuspecting, was asleep in a secret room in my lodgings, they broke
in with the help of one of my servants, whom they had bribed. There
they had vengeance on me with a most cruel and most shameful
punishment, such as astounded the whole world, for they cut off
those parts of my body with which I had done that which was the
cause of their sorrow. This done, straightway they fled, but two of

them were captured, and suffered the loss of their eyes and their genital organs. One of these two was the aforesaid servant, who, even while he was still in my service, had been led by his avarice to betray me.

8. André the Chaplain: Courtly Love
Among the Nobility

Lest we make the mistake of considering medieval man as essentially religious in his instincts, this selection or dialogue from André the Chaplain's *Art of Courtly Love* reminds us that he had other preoccupations. André, who lived during the last part of the twelfth century, was chaplain at the court of the Count of Champagne during the years when Countess Marie, the daughter of Eleanor of Acquitaine, was introducing the new vogue of Provençal romantic love to this more northerly noble circle.

As a part of this local literary movement, which included the Arthurian romances composed by Chrétien de Troyes, André produced his book as a kind of Emily Post-like guide to courtly love for this noble society. The result is somewhat surprising, for it shows us a churchman encouraging romantic sensibilities which seem anything but other-worldly in essence. We can also see how this new vogue for "courtesy," as it was called, helped to exalt the position of women in twelfth-century France and to produce a more cultivated ideal of upper-class social behavior. [From *The Art of Courtly Love* by Andreas Capellanus, trans. John J. Parry, in *Records of Civilization: Sources and Studies* (New York: Columbia University Press, 1941), XXXII, 68–72 and 81–83. Copyright 1941 by Columbia University Press. Reprinted with the omission of footnotes by permission of the publisher.]

A Nobleman Speaks with a Noblewoman

If any nobleman seeks the love of a noblewoman, let him try to attract her with these words. After he has got the conversation started, he should open his heart in this fashion:

"So much nobility is apparent in you, and you are distinguished by so much courtesy, that I believe in the presence of Your Pru-

dence I may without fear of censure say all those things that are
lying in my heart waiting to be said. For if men were not permitted
to reveal to ladies, when they wished, the secrets of their hearts, then
love, which men say is the fountain head and source of all good
things, would already have perished utterly, and no man would be
able to help another, and all works of courtesy would be unknown
to mankind."

THE WOMAN SAYS: You are right, and it pleases me greatly to hear you
say it.

THE MAN SAYS: Although in the flesh I rarely come into your presence,
in heart and in spirit I never depart from it, for the continual thought
which I have of you makes me present with you very often and makes
me see constantly with the eyes of the heart that treasure about which
all my attention turns, and it brings me both pains and many solaces.
For what a man desires with all his heart he is always afraid some un-
favorable happening may interfere with. How faithful I am to you and
with what devotion I am drawn to you no words of mine can tell. For
it seems that if the fidelities of every living soul could be gathered
together in a single person, the total would not be so great, by far, as
the faith that prompts me to serve you, and there is nothing so unalterable in my heart as the intention of serving your glory; that would
be glorious to me beyond all else, and I would consider it a great victory
if I could do anything that would be pleasing to you and remain acceptable to Your Grace. Therefore, while I can see you no pain can touch
me, nobody's plottings can disturb me, just the bare sight of the places
which you seem to inhabit, when reflected in the air, provides me with
powerful incentives for living and with many solaces for a lover. But when
I cannot see you with my bodily eye or breathe the air about you, all
the elements round about begin to rise up against me, and all kinds of
torments begin to afflict me, and I can find no pleasure in any solaces
except those deceitful visions that the drowsiness of slumber brings before me when I am asleep. But although sleep deceives me at times with
a false gift, yet I am exceedingly grateful to him because he did see fit
to deceive me with such a sweet and noble misrepresentation. For this
drowsy gift furnishes me a way and a means for keeping alive and pre-
serves me from the wrath of death; this seems to me a very great and
special boon, for there is no use giving medicine to a dead man. But so
long as I retain life, even though it may be a painful one, the light air
can drench me with a shower of release or cover me with the waters of
gladness. For I believe and have firm confidence that such a noble and
worthy woman will not long permit me to endure such heavy pains, but
will raise me up out of all my difficulties.

THE WOMAN SAYS: Truly in your person good sense has been ennobled and gentle words have found a home, since you can so thoughtfully and so prudently put forward your claims. I am properly grateful that you desire to think of me when I am absent and are determined to be of service to me in every way you can, and I, too, for my part will gladly think of you when you are absent, and I shall not refuse to accept your services at the proper time and place, since you are so great and so eminent a man of worth that it would be considered no honor to any woman to refuse them. Nay more, I do not wish you to be content with merely looking at the air, but you can have sight of me with your corporeal vision and look into my face. For I would rather exert myself to give you directions for keeping alive than offer you cause for death or incur the crime of homicide.

THE MAN SAYS: Although in summertime the life of the crops may be prolonged by light showers, they are not saved from the danger of drying up unless they are drenched with rain. You can, in the way you mention, prolong the life of your lover, but cannot free him from serious danger of death. For a relapse seems more serious than the original disease and makes a man die a harder death, and it is worse to do without what we have been given some hope of attaining than what the wish alone prompts us to hope for. Therefore I would rather perish instantly than suffer the perils of death after many agonies. Therefore let Your Prudence consider and examine carefully which seems more to your credit—to give hope to a lover and so save him from the wrath of death and open up to him the road, which he does not know, to all good deeds, or by denying him this hope to close the road to all good deeds and open up the way of death.

THE WOMAN SAYS: Such aid as I can offer you—that is, that you may see me daily with your bodily eye—I have promised you freely, but what you are asking for you can never obtain by any amount of prayers or efforts, for I am firmly resolved with all my heart never to subject myself to the servitude of Venus or endure the torments of lovers. No one can know, unless he has experienced them, how many troubles lovers undergo, for they are exposed to so many pains and wearinesses that no one could learn them except from experience. But although I shall try by every means to avoid falling into Love's snares, I shall never refuse to you, or to any other man who wishes to serve me, the favor of doing so.

THE MAN SAYS: My lady, God forbid that you should persist in this terrible error, for only those women who are known to have joined Love's army are considered worthy of true praise among men and deserve to be mentioned for their worth in the courts of all rulers. What good in the world it does to have anyone do any good deeds unless they take their origin from love I cannot see. Therefore let such beauty and such worth of character as yours tread the paths of love and try its fortunes, for neither the nature nor the character of a thing can be truthfully understood until it has been tried. Only after you have tried it is it proper for you to reject it.

THE WOMAN SAYS: Men find it easy enough to get into Love's court, but difficult to stay there, because of the pains that threaten lovers; while to get out is, because of the desirable acts of love, impossible or nearly so. For after a lover has really entered into the court of Love he has no will either to do or not to do anything except what Love's table sets before him or what may be pleasing to the other lover. Therefore we ought not seek a court of this kind, for one should by all means avoid entering a place which he cannot freely leave. Such a place may be compared to the court of hell, for although the door of hell stands open for all who wish to enter, there is no way of getting out after you are once in. I would rather, therefore, stay in France and be content with a few coppers and have freedom to go where I would, than to be subject to a foreign power, even though I were loaded down with Hungarian silver, because to have so much is to have nothing. I have therefore good reason to hate the palace of Love, so you must look elsewhere for love, brother.

THE MAN SAYS: No one can have a freer choice than not to wish to be separated from that which he desires with all his heart, for anybody ought to be pleased if he cannot help wishing what he desires with all his might, provided only that the thing is one that may be desired. But one can find nothing in the world more desirable than love, since from it comes the doing of every good thing and without it no one would do anything good in the world. It seems, therefore, that you ought to embrace Love's court with both arms, and his palace should not be at all hateful to you.

THE WOMAN SAYS: To fight under Love's protection may seem to anybody else liberty and a thing to lay hold of, but to me it seems the worst kind of servitude, a thing to be avoided at all costs. You are therefore laboring in vain, since the whole world could not move me from my position.

THE MAN SAYS: If you choose to walk that path, unbearable torments will follow you, the like of which cannot be found and which it would be difficult to tell about.

*   *   *

[THE MAN THEN ADDS:] Know, then, that the chief rules in love are these twelve that follow:

I. Thou shalt avoid avarice like the deadly pestilence and shalt embrace its opposite.

II. Thou shalt keep thyself chaste for the sake of her whom thou lovest.

III. Thou shalt not knowingly strive to break up a correct love affair that someone else is engaged in.

IV. Thou shalt not choose for thy love anyone whom a natural sense of shame forbids thee to marry.

V. Be mindful completely to avoid falsehood.

VI. Thou shalt not have many who know of thy love affair.

VII. Being obedient in all things to the commands of ladies, thou shalt ever strive to ally thyself to the service of Love.

VIII. In giving and receiving love's solaces let modesty be ever present.

IX. Thou shalt speak no evil.

X. Thou shalt not be a revealer of love affairs.

XI. Thou shalt be in all things polite and courteous.

XII. In practicing the solaces of love thou shalt not exceed the desires of thy lover.

*   *   *

[THE MAN SAYS:] Behold then, my lady, how great is the affliction of those who will not love—to what torments they are subjected, and what glory and honor those have earned who did not close the gates of Love to those who desired to enter—so that you may lay aside your erroneous opinion and be worthy to receive the rewards and to escape the torments I have told you about. For it would be unseemly and a desperate evil were a woman so wise and so beautiful as you to be subjected to such heavy torments or to endure so many perils. Now so far as you are concerned I am free from the task appointed me by Love; but you must be attentive and harken to his precepts that you may be worthy to enter into the glory of his beatitude.

THE WOMAN SAYS: If those things which you say are true, it is a glorious thing to take part in the services of Love and very dangerous to reject his mandates. But whether what you say is true or false, the story of these terrible punishments frightens me so that I do not wish to be a stranger to Love's service; but I would be reckoned among his fellowship and would find myself a dwelling at the southern gate. I must therefore follow in every respect the custom of the ladies at the southern gate and neither reject everybody nor admit everybody who knocks at Love's gate. I shall try, therefore, to find out who is worthy to enter, and having tried him and known him I shall receive him in good faith.

THE MAN SAYS: I give thanks to the most mighty King of Love who has seen fit to change your intention and to banish your dire error. But your statement that you wish to consider whether I should be admitted when I cry at the door of Love's palace seems to me a bitter thing, and your word seems rather harsh; for if you have decided about the worth of my character, you can have no real cause for further deliberation. Yet since it is not easy for all a man's good deeds to become known to everybody, it may be that mine are unknown to you, and so perhaps in view of the state of your knowledge this time for consideration for which you ask would be reasonable. But I have so much confidence in the worthy things I have done and in the justice of Your Nobility, that although the gift I ask for may be delayed, I do not believe that services can long be deprived of their rewards. Therefore may God wish me to feel that my hope is bearing fruit, and may the Divine Power make you think of me when I leave, just as I shall retain in my absence the constant thought of you.

9. Louis IX: Advice to His Son

This document, which may well truly represent St. Louis' advice to his eldest son, Philip III, who succeeded him as king, gives us some insight into medieval French royal government and the attitudes of those who wore the French crown. Though its view of the bases of royal authority is an idealized one and thus seems much too pious for our more modern taste, its verbiage masks some very real concepts of kingship. For instance, Louis IX stresses the role of the king as a dispenser of justice to everyone in his realm—especially the poor and the humble. He reveals his distrust of the venality of those who represented the crown as local administrators. He emphasizes that alliance between the king and the towns which had long given strength to the Capetian house, and he makes clear the role of a king as head of the royal family. To St. Louis then, a king should act as a pious but not subservient protector of the Church, a wise steward of his substance, and last, but not least, a careful administrator and dispenser of justice to his realm. [From *Saint Louis' Advice to His Son*, in *Medieval Civilization*, trans. and eds. Dana Munro and George Clarke Sellery (New York: The Century Company, 1910), pp. 366–75. Copyright 1904–7 by The Century Company.]

1. To his dear first-born son, Philip, greeting, and his father's love.

2. Dear son, since I desire with all my heart that you be well instructed in all things, it is in my thought to give you some advice by this writing. For I have heard you say, several times, that you remember my words better than those of any one else.

3. Therefore, dear son, the first thing I advise is that you fix your whole heart upon God, and love Him with all your strength, for without this no one can be saved or be of any worth.

4. You should, with all your strength, shun everything which you believe to be displeasing to Him. And you ought especially to be resolved not to commit mortal sin, no matter what may happen, and you should permit all your limbs to be hewn off, and suffer every manner of torment, rather than fall knowingly into mortal sin.

5. If our Lord send you any adversity, whether illness or other thing, you should receive it in good patience, and thank Him for it, and be grateful for it, for you ought to believe that He will cause everything to turn out for your good; and likewise you should think that you have well merited it, and more also, should He will it, because you have loved Him but little, and served Him but little, and have done many things contrary to His will.

6. If our Lord send you any prosperity, either health of body or other thing, you ought to thank Him humbly for it, and you ought to be careful that you are not the worse for it, either through pride or anything else, for it is a very great sin to fight against our Lord with His gifts.

7. Dear son, I advise you that you accustom yourself to frequent confession, and that you choose always, as your confessors, men who are upright and sufficiently learned, and who can teach you what you should do and what you should avoid. You should so carry yourself that your confessors and other friends may dare confidently to reprove you and show you your faults.

8. Dear son, I advise you that you listen willingly and devoutly to the services of Holy Church, and, when you are in church, avoid frivolity and trifling, and do not look here and there; but pray to God with lips and heart alike, while entertaining sweet thoughts about Him, and especially at the mass, when the body and blood of our Lord Jesus Christ are consecrated, and for a little time before.

9. Dear son, have a tender pitiful heart for the poor, and for all those whom you believe to be in misery of heart or body, and, according to your ability, comfort and aid them with some alms.

10. Maintain the good customs of your realm, and put down the

bad ones. Do not oppress your people and do not burden them with tolls or *tailles,* except under very great necessity.

11. If you have any unrest of heart, of such a nature that it may be told, tell it to your confessor, or to some upright man who can keep your secret; you will be able to carry more easily the thought of your heart.

12. See to it that those of your household are upright and loyal, and remember the Scripture, which says: *"Elige viros timentes Deum in quibus sit justicia et qui oderint avariciam";* that is to say, "Love those who serve God and who render strict justice and hate covetousness"; and you will profit, and will govern your kingdom well.

13. Dear son, see to it that all your associates are upright, whether clerics or laymen, and have frequent good converse with them; and flee the society of the bad. And listen willingly to the word of God, both in open and in secret; and purchase freely prayers and pardons.

14. Love all good, and hate all evil, in whomsoever it may be.

15. Let no one be so bold as to say, in your presence, words which attract and lead to sin, and do not permit words of detraction to be spoken of another behind his back.

16. Suffer it not that any ill be spoken of God or His saints in your presence, without taking prompt vengeance. But if the offender be a clerk or so great a person that you ought not to try him, report the matter to him who is entitled to judge it.

17. Dear son, give thanks to God often for all the good things He has done for you, so that you may be worthy to receive more, in such a manner that if it please the Lord that you come to the burden and honor of governing the kingdom, you may be worthy to receive the sacred unction wherewith the kings of France are consecrated.

18. Dear son, if you come to the throne, strive to have that which befits a king, that is to say, that in justice and rectitude you hold yourself steadfast and loyal toward your subjects and your vassals, without turning either to the right or to the left, but always straight, whatever may happen. And if a poor man have a quarrel with a rich man, sustain the poor rather than the rich, until the truth is made clear, and when you know the truth, do justice to them.

19. If any one have entered into a suit against you (for any injury or wrong which he may believe that you have done to him), be always for him and against yourself in the presence of your council, without showing that you think much of your case (until the truth be made known concerning it); for those of your council might be backward in speaking against you, and this you should not wish;

and command your judges that you be not in any way upheld more than any others, for thus will your councillors judge more boldly according to right and truth.

20. If you have anything belonging to another, either of yourself or through your predecessors, if the matter is certain, give it up without delay, however great it may be, either in land or money or otherwise. If the matter is doubtful, have it inquired into by wise men, promptly and diligently. And if the affair is so obscure that you cannot know the truth, make such a settlement, by the counsel of upright men, that your soul, and the souls of your predecessors, may be wholly freed from the affair. And even if you hear some one say that your predecessors made restitution, make diligent inquiry to learn if anything remains to be restored; and if you find that such is the case, cause it to be delivered over at once, for the liberation of your soul and the souls of your predecessors.

21. You should seek earnestly how your vassals and your subjects may live in peace and rectitude beneath your sway; likewise, the good towns and the good cities of your kingdom. And preserve them in the estate and the liberty in which your predecessors kept them, and if there be anything to amend, amend and redress it, and preserve their favor and their love. For it is by the strength and the riches of your good cities and your good towns that the native and the foreigner, especially your peers and your barons, are deterred from doing ill to you. I will remember that Paris and the good towns of my kingdom aided me against the barons, when I was newly crowned.

22. Honor and love all the people of Holy Church, and be careful that no violence be done to them, and that their gifts and alms, which your predecessors have bestowed upon them, be not taken away or diminished. And I wish here to tell you what is related concerning King Philip, my ancestor, as one of his council, who said he heard it, told it to me. The king, one day, was with his privy council, and he was there who told me these words. And one of the king's councillors said to him how much wrong and loss he suffered from those of Holy Church, in that they took away his rights and lessened the jurisdiction of his court; and they marveled greatly how he endured it. And the good king answered: "I am quite certain that they do me much wrong, but when I consider the goodnesses and kindnesses which God has done me, I had rather that my rights should go, than have a contention or awaken a quarrel with Holy Church." And this I tell to you that you may not lightly believe anything against the people of Holy Church; so love

them and honor them and watch over them that they may in peace do the service of our Lord.

23. Moreover, I advise you to love dearly the clergy, and, so far as you are able, do good to them in their necessities, and likewise love those by whom God is most honored and served, and by whom the Faith is preached and exalted.

24. Dear son, I advise that you love and reverence your father and your mother, willingly remember and keep their commandments, and be inclined to believe their good counsels.

25. Love your brothers, and always wish their well-being and their good advancement, and also be to them in the place of a father, to instruct them in all good. But be watchful lest, for the love which you bear to one, you turn aside from right doing, and do to the others that which is not meet.

26. Dear son, I advise you to bestow the benefices of Holy Church which you have to give, upon good persons, of good and clean life, and that you bestow them with the high counsel of upright men. And I am of the opinion that it is preferable to give them to those who hold nothing of Holy Church, rather than to others. For, if you inquire diligently, you will find enough of those who have nothing who will use wisely that entrusted to them.

27. Dear son, I advise you that you try with all your strength to avoid warring against any Christian man, unless he have done you too much ill. And if wrong be done you, try several ways to see if you can find how you can secure your rights, before you make war; and act thus in order to avoid the sins which are committed in warfare.

28. And if it fall out that it is needful that you should make war (either because some one of your vassals has failed to plead his case in your court, or because he has done wrong to some church or to some poor person, or to any other person whatsoever, and is unwilling to make amends out of regard for you, or for any other reasonable cause), whatever the reason for which it is necessary for you to make war, give diligent command that the poor folk who have done no wrong or crime be protected from damage to their vines, either through fire or otherwise, for it were more fitting that you should constrain the wrongdoer by taking his own property (either towns or castles, by force of siege), than that you should devastate the property of poor people. And be careful not to start the war before you have good counsel that the cause is most reasonable, and before you have summoned the offender to make amends, and have waited as long as you should. And if he ask mercy, you ought to pardon

him, and accept his amende, so that God may be pleased with you.

29. Dear son, I advise you to appease wars and contentions, whether they be yours or those of your subjects, just as quickly as may be, for it is a thing most pleasing to our Lord. And Monsignore St. Martin gave us a very great example of this. For, one time, when our Lord made it known to him that he was about to die, he set out to make peace between certain clerks of his archbishopric, and he was of the opinion that in so doing he was giving a good end to his life.

30. Seek diligently, most sweet son, to have good *baillis* and good *prévôts* in your land, and inquire frequently concerning their doings, and how they conduct themselves, and if they administer justice well, and do no wrong to any one, nor anything which they ought not do. Inquire more often concerning those of your household than of any others, and learn if they be too covetous or too arrogant; for it is natural that the members should seek to imitate their chief; that is, when the master is wise and well-behaved, all those of his household follow his example and prefer it. For however much you ought to hate evil in others, you should have more hatred for the evil which comes from those who derive their power from you, than you bear to the evil of others; and the more ought you to be on your guard and prevent this from happening.

31. Dear son, I advise you always to be devoted to the Church of Rome, and to the sovereign pontiff, our father, and to bear him the reverence and honor which you owe to your spiritual father.

32. Dear son, freely give power to persons of good character, who know how to use it well, and strive to have wickednesses expelled from your land, that is to say, nasty oaths, and everything said or done against God or our Lady or the saints. In a wise and proper manner put a stop, in your land, to bodily sins, dicing, taverns, and other sins. Put down heresy so far as you can, and hold in especial abhorrence Jews, and all sorts of people who are hostile to the Faith, so that your land may be well purged of them, in such manner as, by the sage counsel of good people, may appear to you advisable.

33. Further the right with all your strength. Moreover, I admonish you that you strive most earnestly to show your gratitude for the benefits which our Lord has bestowed upon you, and that you may know how to give Him thanks therefor.

34. Dear son, take care that the expenses of your household are reasonable and moderate, and that its moneys are justly obtained. And there is one opinion that I deeply wish you to entertain, that is to say, that you keep yourself free from foolish expenses and evil

exactions, and that your money should be well expended and well acquired. And this opinion, together with other opinions which are suitable and profitable, I pray that our Lord may teach you.

35. Finally, most sweet son, I conjure and require you that, if it please our Lord that I should die before you, you have my soul succored with masses and orisons, and that you send through the congregations of the kingdom of France, and demand their prayers for my soul, and that you grant me a special and full part in all the good deeds which you perform.

36. In conclusion, dear son, I give you all the blessings which a good and tender father can give to a son, and I pray our Lord Jesus Christ, by His mercy, by the prayers and merits of His blessed Mother, the Virgin Mary, and of angels and archangels and of all the saints, to guard and protect you from doing anything contrary to His will, and to give you grace to do it always, so that He may be honored and served by you. And this may He do to me as to you, by His great bounty, so that after this mortal life we may be able to be together with Him in the eternal life, and see Him, love Him, and praise Him without end. Amen. And glory, honor, and praise be to Him who is one God with the Father and the Holy Spirit; without beginning and without end. Amen.

Part Three
ENGLAND

10. Peter of Blois: A View of England During the Reigns of William Rufus and Henry I

Peter of Blois (1070–1117?), who wrote the following account of England and the Abbey of Croyland during the reigns of William II and Henry I, was continuing a chronicle composed by Ingulf which is often, somewhat unfairly, considered spurious. There can, however, be no doubt as to the authenticity of Peter's continuation of Ingulf's narrative. In it he gives us a view of the tyrannical reign of William Rufus, which bore heavily upon the churches and abbeys of Britain. We also see how an English abbot of the period was chosen by the king and how he went about raising money to repair his ruined monastery by soliciting funds from noble and royal donors from all over Western Europe. Wide-scale fund raising for a good cause, then, represents no modern invention, but was well-known already during the Middle Ages. [From *Ingulf's Chronicle of the Abbey of Croyland with the Continuation of Peter of Blois*, trans. Henry T. Riley (London: Henry G. Bohn, 1854), pp. 229–37.]

William Rufus reigning over the land, and having with a powerful arm conquered all his adversaries, so much so as to have brought all his foes beneath the yoke, while there was no one who dared in any way to murmur against his sway, Ranulph, the bishop of Durham, was his especial adviser in affairs of state. This Ranulph proved a most cruel extortioner, and being the most avaricious and most abandoned of all men in the land, woefully oppressed the

65

whole kingdom, and wrung it even to the drawing of blood; while at the same time Anselm, the most holy archbishop of Canterbury who had succeeded Lanfranc, dragging out a weary existence in exile beyond sea, mercy and truth with him had taken to flight from out of the land, and justice and peace had been banished therefrom. Confession and the fair graces of repentance fell into disesteem, holiness and chastity utterly sickened away, sin stalked in the streets with open and undaunted front, and facing the law with haughty eye, daily triumphed, exulting in her abominable success.

Wherefore, the heavens did abominate the land, and, fighting against sinners, the sun and the moon stood still in their abode, and spurning the earth with the greatest noise and fury, caused all nations to be amazed at their numerous portents. For there were thunders terrifying the earth, lightnings and thunderbolts most frequent, deluging showers without number, winds of the most astonishing violence, and whirlwinds that shook the towers of churches and levelled them with the ground. On the earth there were fountains flowing with blood, and mighty earthquakes, while the sea, overflowing its shores, wrought infinite calamities to the maritime places. There were murders and dreadful seditions; the Devil himself was seen bodily appearing in many woods; there was a most shocking famine, and a pestilence so great among men, as well as beasts of burden, that agriculture was almost totally neglected, as well as all care of the living, all sepulture of the dead.

The limit and termination at last of so many woes, was the death of the king, a cause, to every person of Christian feelings, of extreme grief. For there had come from Normandy, to visit king William, a very powerful baron, Walter Tirel by name. The king received him with the most lavish hospitality, and having honored him with a seat at his table, was pleased, after the banquet was concluded, to give him an invitation to join him in the sport of hunting. After the king had pointed out to each person his fixed station, and the deer, alarmed at the barking of the dogs and the cries of the huntsmen, were swiftly flying towards the summits of the hills, the said Walter incautiously aimed an arrow at a stag, which missed the stag, and pierced the king in the breast.

The king fell to the earth, and instantly died; upon which, the body being laid by a few countrymen in a cart, was carried back to the palace, and on the morrow was buried, with but few manifestations of grief, and in an humble tomb; for all his servants were busily attending to their own interests, and few or none cared for the royal funeral. The said Walter, the author of his death, though unwittingly so, escaped from the midst of them, crossed the sea, and arrived safe home in Normandy.

William was succeeded on the throne by his brother Henry, a young man of extreme beauty, and, from his acquaintance with literature, much more astute than his two brothers, and better fitted for reigning: his brother Robert being at this time in the Holy Land, most valiantly fighting in the army of the Christians against the Turks and Saracens. He was crowned by Thomas, the archbishop of York, because, at this period, Anselm, archbishop of Canterbury, was in exile. Receiving royal homage and the oaths of fealty from all, he immediately gave liberty to the Holy Church, and forbade depraved customs and injurious exactions to prevail; besides which, he threw the said Ranulph, who was the author of them, into prison, and, dispatching a messenger, recalled the most holy archbishop Anselm from exile.

Led astray and seduced by the bad counsels of the said most wicked Ranulph, king William, on the day of his death, held in his own hands the archbishopric of Canterbury, besides four other bishoprics, and eleven abbeys, all of which were let out to farm. He was the first of all the kings who placed the receipts on account of rent of all the vacant churches in his treasury; whereas his father invariably, and with the greatest piety, in the same manner as all the other kings of England, his predecessors, had been in the habit of repaying all rents and profits of that nature, in the case of vacant churches, to the prelates who were the first to succeed, and had to the very last farthing accounted, through faithful servants, for the whole thereof. But as for him, after keeping all these dignities for a long time in his own hands for no good reason whatever, and frequently making grants of them to farmers and usurious Jews, under colour of employing long deliberation in the choice of a proper pastor, he repeatedly put them up to auction among the most ambitious and most wealthy of the clergy; and at last, on finding a well-filled purse as the result, asserting that all sanctity lay in that, he openly declared that that was the only deserving prelate. In this state of things, it was a matter greatly to be commended that, being confined to his bed and almost despairing of his life, on the decease of Lanfranc, the venerable archbishop of Canterbury, a man of most holy life, as well as skilled in all branches of literature, he appointed the venerable Anselm, abbat of Bec, in Normandy, to the archbishopric of Canterbury, in a devout manner, and without any imputation of simony.

The before-named Ranulph, however, made his escape by certain

iniquitous means from prison, and repaired to Normandy, and in
every way encouraged the duke thereof, Robert, the king's brother,
who on hearing of the death of his brother William had immediately
returned from the Holy Land, to invade England. Accordingly, after
the duke had levied a large army, and had come to the sea-shore,
while the king, on the other hand, had strengthened the southern
coasts of his kingdom with troops innumerable (being determined,
once for all, to conquer and reign, or else to lose the kingdom and
perish), archbishop Anselm and other men of character, who were
promoters of peace, acting as mediators between them, brought about
an arrangement upon the following terms; that the king should pay
each year a compensation of three thousand pounds of silver, and
that lasting peace should thenceforth be established between them.
However, in after years, the duke, ill-advisedly, forgave this annual
payment; and besides, he acted unwisely towards the natives [of
Normandy], and those subject to him; upon which the king repaired
to Normandy, and taking his brother prisoner in a pitched battle,
kept him in prison to the day of his death, and united the whole of
Normandy to his own kingdom.

The king, having gained this victory, and being instructed by the
repeated exhortations of the holy archbishop Anselm, remitted for
ever his right of investiture of churches by ring and pastoral staff,
a question which had for a long time harassed the Holy Church;
while he retained in his own hand and excepted solely his royal
privileges. This I think is enough as to the kings.

In these days also, the temporal powers militant, under the command of Godfrey and Baldwin, the most illustrious sons of Eustace,
earl of Boulogne, Robert, duke of Normandy, and Raymond, earl of
Toulouse, together with Boamund, duke of Apulia, and their armies
and troops from the rest of Christendom, having subjugated all
Lycia, Mesopotamia, and at last the whole of Syria, rendered subject
to their dominion and to the Christian faith, first, the city of
Nicca, then Antioch, and after that, holy Jerusalem.

At this time also, the spiritual powers militant of the monastic
order, springing up from the monastery of Molisme, sent forth so
many offshoots, that, through its first-born daughter of Cisteaux, at
this day innumerable monasteries, abodes of the servants of God,
exist, which were produced by the Divine power under their original
fathers, Robert, Alberic, Stephen, and Bernard; from the last of
whom an idea may be formed as to the multitude of the rest. For
the said father Saint Bernard saw sons of his go forth from his
monastery of Clairvaux, over which he presided for the space of

forty years, one as pope of the see of Rome, to wit, Eugenius, two as cardinals, and sixteen as archbishops and bishops in different parts of the world; of whom we had one at York in England, archbishop Henry, and two in Ireland, who proved themselves Christians both in name and deed; together with two hundred monasteries and more which he produced from his own of Clairvaux, and which themselves were daily bringing forth others innumerable unto the Lord.

At this period also, the venerable Ingulph, the lord abbat of Croyland, was greatly afflicted by multiplied maladies which wearied and harassed his declining years to such a degree, that he was unable to continue the history of his monastery to the close of his life: for many are the inconveniences which surround the aged man. Nevertheless, after he had laboured most zealously in the restoration of his house, which had been lately destroyed by fire, and in the rebuilding of his church, as well as in replacing the books, vestments, bells, and other requisites, the old man, having served his time in the warfare of this life, and being full of days, departed unto the Lord; after having completed thirty-four years in the most laborious discharge of his pastoral duties as sole abbat, during ten of which abbat Wulketul, his predecessor, was still surviving; while, during the remaining twenty-four years he was much harassed and annoyed by the adversaries of the monastery, as well as by other misfortunes, but had been always wonderously supported by the Lord. At last, however, bidding farewell to the maliciousness of the world, he was received in Abraham's bosom with all the Saints, being thus relieved from the affliction of gout, under which, in his later years, he had languished, and received to the eternal joys of Paradise, on the sixteenth day before the calends of January, in the year of our Lord, 1109, being the ninth year of the reign of king Henry. He was buried in his chapter-house, on the feast of Saint Thomas the Apostle.

At the repeated suggestion and frequent entreaties of Alan Croun, who was Seneschal of the royal mansion, and dear to the king beyond all the other barons of the palace, and admitted to all his counsels (being a man who excelled all others in industry and probity, in wisdom and sanctity, so much so, that by his fellow-knights he was called "the King's God"), king Henry following his advice, invited from the monastery of Saint Evroult in Normandy, Joffrid, the lord prior of the said place, who was closely related to the said most illustrious Seneschal of the royal palace. This he did by his epistle directed to the venerable father Manerius, the abbat of the said monastery, in which he invited the said venerable man, the prior Joffrid, noble in the flesh, but much more noble in spirit. For he was the son of the marquis Herebert, by Hildeburga, sister of Guido Croun, the father of the before-named Alan, but was born and educated at Orleans, and from his infancy destined by his parents for a monastic life: him, on the death of Ingulph, the venerable abbat of Croyland, the king most beneficially appointed in his place, as pastor of the said monastery. The abbacy had been vacant at this time for the space of three months and a few days, the king, after the most abominable example of his brother William, continuing to hold it during the vacancy; still, through his affection for the said Alan, he liberally and in full paid over to the said abbat, on his appointment, all the profits that he had received.

The said venerable abbat Joffrid arrived at Croyland on Palm Sunday, C being the Dominical letter, and was joyously received. Immediately passing thence to Lincoln, he received the blessing from bishop Robert in his chapel there, and was installed on the Lord's day, upon which *"Quasi modi geniti"* is sung. That he might not at the beginning be looked upon as a useless pastor, or as sluggish and pusillanimous, he began to look about him on every side in his monastery, and, as well became a man of such a character, did not indulge himself in snoring in bed, or lying concealed; but in private taught in mild accents the masters of the earth to fear God, while in public he reverently besought the people subject to him, devoutly to pray on all occasions, at the entreaties of the priests expounded the Holy Gospel, and in all his discourses ever preferred the honor of God and the saving of souls, far before all things temporal.

For he was more learned than any of his predecessors, abbats of Croyland, having imbibed literature of every description with his mother's milk from his very cradle. Seeing his convent, which still remained half burnt, and had been plucked like a brand from the burning, in some measure rebuilt, but still in a hasty manner, and far from replaced in becoming splendour and restored to its proper vigour, he resolved to found a new church, and to rebuild the whole monastery with walls of stone instead of walls of clay, and upon a marble foundation, if his means would allow thereof.

First sitting down, therefore, and calculating the necessary outlay, on examining the whole of the substance of his monastery, he found that it would by no means suffice for a work of such magnitude; upon which, in order that the words used by our Lord, "This man began to build and was not able to finish," might not be said of him, he obtained of the venerable archbishops of Canterbury and York and the other bishops of England, their suffragans, an indulgence of a third part of the penance enjoined for sins committed, the same being graciously granted to every one who should be a benefactor of his monastery, and should assist in the promotion of the works of the church. Thus, if in a week a fast of three days was imposed upon any persons for the punishment of their sins, a penance of one day was by the said indulgence remitted; and again, if two days' penance were imposed upon any person by the Penancer, that for one of them was remitted.

Having obtained this indulgence, he now opened the foundation of his new church, and sent throughout the whole of England, and into the lands adjoining beyond sea, letters testimonial of the said indulgence, entreating all the faithful in Christ to give their kind assistance for the promotion of his undertaking, granting in return to every one who should assist him the favour of the aforesaid indulgence in presence of God. In order zealously to carry out the same, he sent the venerable men, brothers Ægelmer and Nigel, his fellow-monks, with relics of the Saints, into the western parts, namely, Flanders and France. To the northern parts and into Scotland he sent the brothers Fulk and Oger, and into Denmark and Norway the brothers Swetman and Wulsin the younger; while to Wales, Cornwall, and Ireland he sent the brothers Augustin and Osbert. All of these were his brother-monks, industrious men, most prompt and ready, and well fitted to carry out such a work; these he sent with letters recommendatory directed to the kings and princes of countries and provinces, to the following effect:

"To the most illustrious————, by the grace of God (king of the Franks, Scots, or the like, as the case might be), the earls, barons, archbishops, bishops, abbats, priors, as also to all rulers of churches, and their priests and clerks, and to all the faithful of Christ in the kingdom to them subject, and to the rich and poor brethren living under their rule, Joffrid, abbat of the Church of God and of the glorious Mary, ever a Virgin, and of Saint Bartholomew the Apostle and of the most holy Guthlac the Confessor, the son of noble kings, and of Saint Waldev, the late Martyr, and of the whole convent of the brethren entrusted unto him by God, the everlasting blessing Apostolical and ecclesiastical from our Lord Jesus Christ and from ourselves. O sirs, and would that it may prove most true friends of God, night and day for our sins and those of all Christians, and in especial for all who do good unto us, do we cheerfully serve those whose names we have written above; that is to say, our Lord Jesus

Christ and His glorious Mother, Saint Bartholomew the Apostle, the holy Confessor Guthlac, and Waldev, the late holy Martyr. Know, O sirs, and friends of God, that we have lately levelled to the ground the church of the friends of God, whom we have named, inasmuch as it greatly threatened to fall; but the same now lies immersed in quagmires, and of ourselves we are not able to rebuild it, unless the good and kind Jesus, through you and others of His people, shall grant us His assistance. We do therefore direct unto your dignity these our humble letters, to the end that your most powerful aid may come to our assistance, and that we may be enabled to re-erect the church of God and of His Saints. It is also profitable and becoming that you should hear what reward you will in this world receive at the hands of God. We are living under the royal sway of the English land; and unto the two archbishops, besides other bishops, the holy Church is subject in all matters of holy ordinance. In these the Divine goodness has inspired such love towards us, in the extreme affection which they entertain towards our said Church, that they have remitted to penitents the third part of their penance, and together with us take the same on themselves; that is to say, if a fast of three days in the week has been imposed on a sinner, one of them is to be remitted to him, and one mass is to be celebrated for him; and if a fast of two days has been imposed on him, still, one is to be remitted to him, and in like manner, mass is to be celebrated for him; and further, twelve poor shall every day be relieved on behalf of those who give aid to our church. Farewell."

Moreover, the before-named monks, in strenuously carrying out the duties enjoined on them, not only brought worldly substance and perishable money to their church, but also conducted many souls unto heaven, as well as induced the bodies of some to enter the monastic order, not only among the natives but among foreigners as well.

11. Henry of Huntingdon: The Disorders of Stephen's Reign

The years between the death of Henry I in 1135 and the accession of Henry II in 1154 were melancholy ones in England; Stephen attempted to rule as king while he was opposed by his formidable cousin, the Empress Matilda. The Empress Matilda was the daughter of Henry I and the mother of Henry II, while Stephen was a son of Adele, the sister of Henry I. Taking advantage of the ensuing civil war, the nobility seized control of vast areas of Britain, extorted concessions from both parties in the civil strife, raised illegal castles, and oppressed both the Church and the general populace.

Some idea of what all this represented for the realm can be seen in the following account by Henry, Archdeacon of Huntingdon, who was born shortly after 1080 and lived until the early years of Henry II's reign. Particularly significant seems to be his account of how Geoffrey and Stephen de Mandeville and other magnates like them took advantage of the situation to gain authority for themselves by every possible means. One should also note the role played by mercenary soldiers and town militias during these years of disorder, a role which many earlier authorities, overstressing the feudal levy, have tended to underestimate. [From *The Chronicle of Henry of Huntingdon*, trans. Thomas Forester (London: Henry G. Bohn, 1853; George Bell and Sons, 1876), pp. 400–409.]

At this period England was in a very disturbed state; on the one hand, the king and those who took his part grievously oppressed the people, on the other frequent turmoils were raised by the Earl of Gloucester,[1] and, what with the tyranny of the one, and the turbulence of the other, there was universal turmoil and desolation. Some, for whom their country had lost its charms, chose rather to make their abode in foreign lands; others drew to the churches for protection, and constructing mean hovels in their precincts, passed their days in fear and trouble. Food being scarce, for there was a dreadful famine throughout England, some of the people disgustingly devoured the flesh of dogs and horses; others appeased their insatiable hunger with the garbage of uncooked herbs and roots; many, in all parts, sunk under the severity of the famine and died in heaps; others with their whole families went sorrowfully into voluntary banishment and disappeared. There were seen famous cities deserted and depopulated by the death of the inhabitants of every age and sex, and fields white for the harvest, for it was near the season of autumn, but none to gather it, all having been struck down by the famine. Thus the whole aspect of England presented a scene of calamity and sorrow, misery and oppression. It tended to increase the evil, that a crowd of fierce strangers who had flocked to England in bands to take service in the wars, and who

[1] [One of England's leading nobles, who used the disorders of this period to make himself all but independent of the crown, though officially he was a backer of Matilda—Ed.]

were devoid of all bowels of mercy and feelings of humanity, were scattered among the people thus suffering. In all the castles their sole business was to contrive the most flagitious outrages; and the employment on which all the powers of their malicious minds were bent, was to watch every opportunity of plundering the weak, to foment troubles, and cause bloodshed in every direction. And as the barons who had assembled them from the remotest districts were neither able to discharge their pay out of their own revenues, nor to satisfy their insatiable thirst for plunder, and remunerate them by pillage as they had before done, because there was nothing left anywhere whole and undamaged, they had recourse to the possessions of the monasteries, or the neighbouring municipalities, or any others which they could send forth troops enough to infest. At one time they loaded their victims with false accusations and virulent abuse; at another they ground them down with vexatious claims and extortions; some they stripped of their property, either by open robbery or secret contrivance, and others they reduced to complete subjection in the most shameless manner. If any one of the reverend monks, or of the secular clergy, came to complain of the exactions laid on church property, he was met with abuse, and abruptly silenced with outrageous threats; the servants who attended him on his journey were often severely scourged before his face, and he himself, whatever his rank and order might be, was shamefully stripped of his effects, and even his garments, and driven away, or left helpless, from the severe beating to which he was subjected. These unhappy spectacles, these lamentable tragedies, as they were common throughout England, could not escape the observation of the bishops. But they, bowed down by base fears, like reeds before the wind, their salt having lost its savour, did not rear themselves like a tower of strength for the protection of the House of Israel. They ought, indeed, to have opposed these carnal men with the sword of the Spirit, which destroys the flesh; and to have resolutely set their face like Jeremiah, or like the radiant brow of Moses, against the sons of Belial, who plundered the church, and, tearing in pieces the garment of the Lord, left it rent and torn and scattered everywhere. The bishops are figured by the columns on which the house of God was built, by the lions which supported the laver of Solomon, by the pillars on which stood the table of shew-bread; inasmuch as it is their duty to be not only the support and bulwark, but the strong defence, against all enemies of the church; which is truly the house of God, which is represented in the laver, because there all the guilt of sinners is washed away, and is figured by the table, because on that the bread of eternal life is offered. Far from this, when robbers laid violent hands on the possessions of the church, as I have often related, the bishops, some, yielding to their fears, either acquiesced or pronounced with mildness and hesitation the sentence of excommunication, quickly withdrawn; others, not indeed acting as became bishops, victualled their castles and filled them with men-at-arms and archers, under pretence of restraining the marauders and robbers of churches, while they proved themselves more inhuman, more merciless, than those sons of violence in oppressing their neighbours and pillaging their property. The bishops themselves, shameful to say, not all indeed, but several of them, assumed arms, and, girt with the sword and sheathed in bright armour, rode on mettlesome war-horses beside the ravagers of the country, received their share of the booty, and subjected to imprisonment and torture soldiers who fell into their hands by chance of war, and men of wealth wherever they met with them; and while they were at the bottom of all this flagitious wickedness, they ascribed it not to themselves, but to their soldiers only. To be silent for the present, respecting others, for it would be wrong to accuse all alike, common report stigmatized the Bishops of Winchester, Lincoln, and Chester, as more forward than others in these unchristian doings. . . .

[W]hen the Earl of Hereford, being in much want of money to pay the troops which he had levied against the king, forced the churches in his lordship to submit to new exactions, and required the Bishop of Hereford to pay the tax tyrannically imposed, claiming it as his right, and enforcing it by threats; being thus frequently pressed, the bishop deliberately and positively refused to pay the demand, asserting that ecclesiastical property, assigned to the altar by the pious offerings of devout people, belonged, in perpetual frankalmoin, to the service of God and the church, and that no layman could interfere with them, any more than he could in the sacred rites; so that by laying hands on them he incurred the guilt of sacrilege, as much as if he had violated the altar itself. Wherefore, he required the earl to withdraw his presumptuous demand, and to restrain his people, or he threatened him and them with immediate excommunication.

This resolution of the bishop inflamed Milo to the highest pitch of rage, and he sent his followers to seize the bishop's goods and lands, and lay them waste wherever they were. Upon which the bishop, assembling his clergy, who willingly attended his summons, pronounced the terrible sentence of excommunication against Milo and his adherents. He further layed an interdict on the whole country which was subject to Milo, by the rigour of which it was prohibited that any of the sacred offices of the church should be performed, and no corpse was to be buried in the earth, or committed to the waters, or consumed by fire, or removed from the place where it expired, until the author of the sacrilege restored all that he had seized, to the last farthing as valued by sworn men, and, doing penance, was reconciled to the church. But as after he had promised to make restitution, the jury had to take an account, so that while satisfaction was made to one church, others were injured by delay, and their ministers were involved in pleadings between themselves and the bishop, he perished miserably within the year, without receiving absolution; having been pierced through the breast with an arrow shot by a soldier at a stag, while the earl was hunting deer on Christmas eve. His death struck the covetous with some alarm, and restrained them from laying hands so freely on church property; and it made the other bishops bolder in afterwards resisting such sacrilegious attempts. Roger, Milo's son, succeeded him in the earldom of Hereford, and, young as he was, displayed great abilities.

There was, at this time, among the king's adherents, one Geoffrey de Mandeville, a man remarkable for his great prudence, his inflexible spirit in adversity, and his military skill. His wealth and his honours raised him above all the nobles of the realm; for he held the Tower of London, and had built castles of great strength round the city, and in every part of the kingdom which submitted to the king; being everywhere the king's representative, so that in public affairs he was more attended to than the king himself, and the royal commands were less obeyed than his own. This occasioned jealousy, particularly among those who were familiarly and intimately connected with the king, as Geoffrey, it appeared, had managed to usurp all the rights of the king: and, moreover, report said that he was inclined to confer the crown on the Countess of Anjou. They, therefore, secretly persuaded the king to arrest Geoffrey on the charge of treason, and to obtain the forfeiture of his castles, for his own security and his kingdom's peace. The king hesitated for some time, being unwilling to involve the royal majesty in the disgrace of false accusations, when a sudden strife arose between Geoffrey and the barons, in which abuse and menaces were exchanged between the parties. The king interfered to settle the dispute, but while he was endeavouring to do so, some persons came forward and accused Geoffrey boldly of a conspiracy against the king and his party. Instead of taking the least pains to clear himself of the charge, he treated it with ridicule, as an infamous falsehood; whereupon the king and the barons present arrested him and his followers. This happened at St. Alban's.

The king brought Geoffrey to London in close custody, and threatened to hang him if he did not give up the Tower of London, and the castles he had erected with wonderful skill and labour. By the advice of his friends, to escape an ignominious death, he submitted to the king's will, and agreed to the surrender; and being thus set at liberty, he escaped out of the hands of his enemies, to the great injury of the whole kingdom. For, being turbulent and fierce, by the exercise of his power he gave strength to rebellion through all England; as the king's enemies, hearing that he was in arms against the royal cause, and relying on the support of so great an earl, began, with new spirit, to raise insurrections in every quarter; and even those who appeared to be the king's supporters, as if they had been struck by a thunderbolt, were more and more humiliated by his secession from the king's party.

Geoffrey now assembled all his dependents, who were bound to him by fealty and homage, in one body, and he also levied a formidable host of mercenary soldiers and of freebooters, who flocked to him gladly from all quarters. With this force he devastated the whole country by fire and sword; driving off flocks and herds with insatiable cupidity, sparing neither age nor profession, and, freely slaking his thirst for vengeance, the most exquisite cruelties he could invent were instantly executed on his enemies. The town of Cambridge, belonging to the king, was taken by surprise, when the citizens were off their guard, and, being plundered, and the doors of the churches being forced with axes, they were pillaged of their wealth, and whatever the citizens had deposited in them; and the town was set on fire. With the same ferocity Geoffrey devastated the whole neighbourhood, breaking into all the churches, desolating the lands of the monks, and carrying off their property. The abbey of St. Benedict, at Ramsey, he not only spoiled of the monks' property, and stripped the altars and the sacred relics, but, mercilessly expelling the monks from the abbey, he placed soldiers in it and made it a garrison.

As soon as the king heard of this bold irruption, and the lawless invasion by Geoffrey of a wide extent of country, he hastened with a powerful array of troops to check the progress of the sudden outbreak. But Geoffrey skilfully avoided an encounter with the king, at one time betaking himself hastily to the marshes, with which that country abounds, where he had before found shelter in his flight; at another, leaving the district where the king was pursuing him, he appeared, at the head of his followers, in another quarter, to stir up fresh disturbances. However, for the purpose of checking his usual inroads into that country, the king caused castles to be built in suitable places, and placing garrisons in them, to overawe the marauders, he went elsewhere to attend to other affairs. As soon as the king was gone, Geoffrey devoted all his energies to reduce the garrisons which the king had left for his annoyance, supported by the king's enemies, who flocked to him from all quarters; and, forming a confederacy with Hugh Bigod, a man of note, who was very powerful in those parts, and had disturbed the peace of the kingdom, and opposed the king's power, as before mentioned, he ravaged the whole country, sparing, in his cruelties, neither sex nor condition. But at length God, the just avenger of all the grievous persecutions, and all the calamities which he had inflicted, brought him to an end worthy of his crimes. For, being too bold, and depending too much on his own address, he often beat up the quarters of the royal garrisons; but at last was outwitted by them and slain; and as while he lived he had disturbed the church, and troubled the land, so the whole English church was a party to his punishment; for, having been excommunicated, he died unabsolved, and the sacrilegious man was deprived of Christian burial.

Such having been the end of Geoffrey [de Mandeville], the prospects of the king's enemies became gloomy; for those who trusted that the royal cause would be much weakened by his secession, now thought that by his death the king would be more at liberty, and, as it turned out, better prepared to molest them. But they set no bounds to the malevolence and impiety with which they were imbued, but, their bad spirit actuating them to every sort of wickedness, they devoted themselves to the prosecution of their rebellion, and engaged, with increased eagerness, in every destructive enterprise through all parts of England. All the northern counties were subject to the tyranny of the Earl of Chester, who subjected the king's barons in the neighbourhood to his yoke, surprised their castles by clandestine assaults, and wasted their lands by hostile incursions; and, breathing in his rage nothing but war and devastation, was the terror of all men. John, also, that child of hell, and root of all evil, the lord of Marlborough Castle, was indefatigable in his efforts to create disturbances. He built castles of strong masonry, on spots he thought advantageous; he got into his power the lands and possessions of the monasteries, expelling the monks of every order; and when the sword of ecclesiastical discipline was unsheathed, he was in no wise deterred, but became still more hardened. He even compelled the monks of the highest order to come to his castle in a body, on certain fixed days, when, assuming episcopal power, he issued irreversible decrees for the payment of taxes, or for compulsory labour. The sons of Robert, earl of Gloucester, also, active young men, and well practised in all military exercises, as well as animated by their father's valour and constancy, kept the south of the kingdom in alarm; building castles in advantageous positions, surprising others held by their neighbours, engaging in frequent expeditions against the enemy, slaying, and plundering, and wasting their lands. With activity like their father's, they had spread their hostilities over a great breadth of country, extending across from one sea to the other, and, having at length acquired the lordship of an ample domain, they affected peace, and promulgated laws and ordinances; but though their vassals might seem relieved from hostilities and pillage, their lords' avarice subjected them to endless taxation, and involved them in vexatious suits.

Stephen de Mandeville, likewise, a man of note, and a persevering soldier, who greatly exalted the earldom of Devon, actively fomented the civil war in those parts. He repaired the old castles, which the necessities of a former age had planted on the summits of precipitous rocks, subjected wide districts to his tyrannical rule, and was a most troublesome neighbour to the king's adherents wherever he established himself. All these, and others whom I omit, not to be tedious, were busily employed in undermining the king's power; and when he was anxiously engaged in allaying these disturbances, sometimes in one quarter, sometimes in another, they would suddenly unite in a body, and vigilantly defeat his designs. In like manner, the royalists, in the several counties of England, attacked the castles whenever a fit opportunity offered, at one time by open hostilities, at another by surprise; so that, by these mutual depredations and alternate excursions and encounters, the kingdom, which was once the abode of joy, tranquillity, and peace, was everywhere changed into a seat of war and slaughter, and devastation and woe.

At that time William de Dover, a skilful soldier, and an active partisan of the Earl of Gloucester, with his support, took possession of Cricklade, a village delightfully situated in a rich and fertile neighbourhood. He built a castle for himself there with great diligence, on a spot which, being surrounded on all sides by waters and marshes, was very inaccessible, and having a strong body of mercenary troops, including some archers, he extended his ravages far and wide, and, reducing to submission a great extent of country on both banks of the river Thames, he inflicted great cruelties on the royal party. At one time fiercely sweeping round their castles in a bold excursion, at another, lurking by night in some concealed ambush, his restless activity never ceased to harass them, and no place could be considered free from danger. Ceaseless as were his efforts to annoy the royalists, the citizens of Oxford and the principal burgesses of the town of Malmesbury, suffered most frequently from his predatory expeditions; because his neighbours in their encounters frequently defeated him. The Earl of Gloucester, also, hastily running up three forts close to Malmesbury, while the king was detained by hostile movements in another direction, was not only able to restrain their usual inroads through the country, but reduced them to famine by his close blockade.

But when the king received exact information of the desperate state of affairs in that quarter, he instantly mustered a large body of troops, and, coming unexpectedly to Malmesbury, threw into it provisions enough to last for a considerable time, and having wasted and pillaged the country round the earl's forts, he encamped near Tetbury, a castle distant three miles from Malmesbury, which he used his utmost endeavours to take. Having stormed the outer defences of the castle, some of the garrison being slain had taken prisoners, and the rest being driven by degrees into a narrow space within the inner court, with many of them wounded, he lost no time in bringing up his war engines with the intention of inclosing and besieging them there. Meanwhile, the Earl of Gloucester, on the first intelligence of the king's coming, gathered an overwhelming force from his numerous castles in the neighbourhood, some his own people, others true to the fealty they owed him. Having increased his army by levying large bodies of foot soldiers, fierce and undisciplined hands of Welshmen, and of recruits drawn from Bristol and other towns in the neighbourhood, he marched to offer the king battle. Roger, earl of Hereford, also, and other powerful barons, with one consent, collected their forces, and speedily joined him, and, advancing within two miles of the royal camp, they lay waiting until other troops who were preparing to join them reinforced the army.

The barons in the king's camp learning that such hordes of the enemy had flocked together to offer them battle, and dreading the headlong rush of the fierce Welsh, and the disorderly crush of the Bristol mob, assembled by the earl in such vast numbers to overwhelm the royal troops, they wisely advised the king to raise the siege, and, for a while, draw off his army, on some other enterprise. They represented that it was rash and dangerous to expose his small band of men-at-arms among such a crowd of butchers, fighting on foot; more especially, as the king's troops were at a great distance from their resources, and were worn by a long march, while, on the contrary, the enemy, assembled from the neighbouring towns and castles, came to the battle in full vigour, fresh from their homes, and with their strength undiminished by sufferings on the road. They, therefore, said that it would be prudent to abandon the siege at present, lest they should suffer a reverse in engaging with the fierce multitudes who now threatened to surround them. The king assented to this judicious advice, and, withdrawing in great haste from that neighbourhood, marched to Winchcombe, arriving unexpectedly before the castle which Roger, the new earl of Hereford, had built there to overawe the royal party. . . .

12. Matthew of Westminster: Simon de Montfort's Rebellion

During the thirteenth century the tradition of a history written by able monkish chroniclers culminated in the writings of a series of important English historians like Matthew of Paris who, in such royal abbeys as St. Albans and Bury St. Edmunds, were able to depict the entire European scene in accurate detail. Such an account is this one composed in the late thirteenth century in the royal abbey of Westminster and ascribed to a certain Matthew. This chronicler, thanks to the location of his house, writes with a special London bias and in the selections which follow, describes the rebellion of English barons led by Simon de Montfort. Historians of the last century were fascinated by this revolt because, due to its temporary success in 1265, Simon was able to summon the first modern type of parliament that represented most segments of the population. The attentive reader of these pages, however, will note that the chronicler does not share modern sympathy with the baronial party and that Parliament's summoning is hardly mentioned— a fact that should warn us that what concerned the nineteenth-century Whig historian, who so frequently viewed the Middle Ages as a part of the nineteenth century, often seems unimportant to the thirteenth-century analyst. [From *The Flowers of History* collected by Matthew of Westminster, trans. C. D. Yonge II (London: Henry G. Bohn, 1853; George Bell and Sons), pp. 414–17 and 436–38.]

Simon de Montfort, the illustrious earl of Leicester, and the barons, having assembled their forces from all quarters, and collected troops, both of the Londoners, whose army had increased to fifteen thousand men, and of men from other parts in countless numbers, marched thither with great impetuosity and courage. Accordingly, they encamped at Flexinge, in Sussex, which is about six miles from Lewes, and three days before the battle, they addressed a message of the following tenor to their lord the king:—

"To the most excellent lord Henry, by the grace of God, king of England, &c. The barons and others, his faithful subjects, wishing to observe their oaths and the fidelity due to God and to him, wish health, and tender their lawful service with all respect and honour. As it is plain from much experience that those who are present with you have suggested to your highness many falsehoods respecting us, intending all the mischief that they can do, not only to you but also to us, and to your whole kingdom, we wish your excellency to know that we wish to preserve the safety and security of your person with all our might, as the fidelity which we owe to you demands, proposing to overthrow, to the utmost of our power, all those who are not our enemies but yours too, and the foes of the whole of your kingdom; and if any other statement is made to you respecting these matters, do not believe it; for we shall always be found your faithful subjects. And we, Simon de Montfort, earl of Leicester, and Gilbert de Clare, at the request of the rest, have, for us and for them too who are here present, affixed our seals. Given at," &c.

But the king, despising this letter from his barons, was eager for war with all his heart, and sent them back the following letter of defiance:—

"Henry, by the grace of God, king of England, &c., to Simon de Montfort and Gilbert de Clare, and their partisans. Since, from the war and general confusion existing in our kingdom, which has all been caused by you, and by the conflagrations and other lawless mischiefs, it is distinctly visible that you do not preserve the fidelity which you owe to us, and that you have in no respect any regard for the safety of our person, since you have wickedly attacked our nobles and others our faithful subjects, who have constantly preserved their fidelity to us, and since you still design to injure them as far as in your power, as you have signified to us by your letters, we consider their grievances as our own, and look upon their enemies as ours; especially since those our faithful subjects before mentioned are manfully standing by us and maintaining their fidelity in opposition to your disloyal conduct, and we do not care for your safety or your affection, but defy you, as the enemies of us and them. Witness my hand, at Lewes, on the twelfth day of May, in the forty-eighth year of our reign."

"Richard, by the grace of God, king of the Romans, always Augustus, and Edward, the illustrious eldest son of the king of England, and all the other barons and nobles who constantly with the labours of sincere good faith and devotedness have adhered to the aforesaid king of England, to Simon de Montfort, Gilbert de Clare, and each and all the others who are accomplices in their treason. By your letters which you have sent to the illustrious king of England, our dearest lord, we understand that we are defied by you, although a verbal defiance of this kind was long ago sufficiently proved to us by actual reality, through your hostile pursuit of us, your burning of our properties, and general devastation of our possessions; we, therefore, wish you to know that you are all defied by each and all of us, as public enemies, and that we are your enemies; and that we will labour with all our might to the damage of your persons and property, whenever any opportunity of injuring either is offered to us. But as to what you falsely charge us with, that we give neither faithful nor salutary counsel to the king your master, you do not at all say the truth; and if you, Simon de Montfort or Gilbert de Clare, choose to assert this same thing in the court of our lord the king, we are prepared to procure a safe conduct and to come to the said court, and to prove the truth of our innocence in this particular, and your falsehood as perfidious traitors, by another who is your equal in nobleness and blood. And we are all content with the seals of the lords above mentioned, namely, of the king of the Romans and the lord Edward. Given as above."

As, therefore, God did by no means admit of their coming to agreement, a most terrible battle took place between them, at Lewes, on the fourteenth of May, such as had never been heard of in past ages. The barons (among whom there was in all things and in every danger but one faith and one will, since they were so unanimous in their fraternal affection that they feared not even to die for their cause,) came the first thing in the morning in front of Lewes, and placed their tents and baggage on a hill, the chariot of the earl of Leicester, with his standard, being carefully placed below under the brow. And so the army and line of battle were arranged, and a speech of great persuasiveness was made to the soldiers by their general, Simon de Montfort, by which all were encouraged, and prepared to fight for their country with every feeling of security. Moreover, all of them having made a confession beforehand, crossed themselves on their shoulders and breasts. Therefore, the king and the other nobles, being informed of their sudden advance, wakened up all through the camp, and speedily assembled in arms, and marshalled their army for battle, arraying a vast multitude of men armed with breastplates; but the greater number of them being false and factious, and destitute of all proper principle, marched forward on that day without any order, and with precipitation, and fought unskilfully, and showed no steady perseverance. And in the actual battle the noblest of the knights and esquires, to the number of about three hundred, lost all courage, and turning their backs, fled to the castle of Peneneselli. Among them, were John, earl of Warrenne, William de Valence, Guy de Lizunac, both the two last being brothers of the king, Hugh Bigod, and many others. But the king's army, which was adorned with the royal standard, which they call the dragon, and which marshalled the way to a fierce contest to the death, advanced forward, and the battle began. For the royal troops rapidly opened their close battalions, and boldly urged their horses against the enemy, and attacked them on the flank. And thus the two armies encountered one another, with fierce blows and horrid noises. Therefore, in this way, the line of battle of the barons was pierced and broken; and John de Giffard, a gallant knight, who had been ambitious to gain the honour of striking the first blow, was taken prisoner, and led away to the castle. But Edward got among the forces of the Londoners, and pursued them when flying, and letting the nobles escape, he followed them, as it is said, for a distance of about four miles, inflicting on them a most lamentable slaughter. For he thirsted for their blood as a punishment for the insult they had offered to his mother, for, as has been already recorded, they had heaped a great deal of abuse on his mother. But a part of the king's army, in the meantime, thirsting for the spoils, and booty, and plunder of the baggage which was on the hills, slew some of the citizens of London, who, for security's sake, had been introduced into the earl's chariot, hoping that they had found the earl himself there. But that earl, and Gilbert de Clare, and the other barons, acting with more sagacity, put forth all their strength to effect the capture of the king of England, and the king of Germany, and the rest of the chiefs. And there the fiery valour of the barons was visibly displayed, who fought eagerly for their country, and at last gained the victory. For the king of England was taken prisoner, after a very

fine horse had been killed under him; and Richard, king of the
Romans, was taken prisoner, and many others were taken also,
namely, John de Balliol, Robert de Bruce, John Comyn, and other
barons of Scotland, and nearly all the men-at-arms whom they had
brought with them from Scotland were slain, to a very great number.

*   *   *

There was but little mention made for a year of the deliverance
of Edward, the king's eldest son, until he himself, as the price of
his release, gave his palatine county of Chester to the aforesaid earl
of Leicester, and thus he purchased his liberation from the imprisonment and custody of the knights, his enemies. No one can adequately relate the condition of the nobles of the Marches, and the
persecutions which they endured for a year and more. But when
the earl of Leicester endeavoured to banish these lords marchers
into Ireland, they, entering the camp of the king's eldest son, on the
extreme borders of Wales, plundered the Welsh castles of their
enemies before mentioned, and thus furnished themselves with
the necessary supplies, until the aforesaid earl of Leicester, having
taken prisoner earl Ferrars, who secretly inclined to the party adverse to the capture of the earl of Gloucester, who has been often
mentioned, and whom they suspected of similar sentiments, came
to Gloucester. For then the lords marchers having united with the
earl of Gloucester to meet their common danger, when the earl of
Warrenne and William de Valence came with a large company of
cross-bowmen and knights and landed in South Wales, they were
inspired with greater boldness to resist the attacks of their persecu-
tors; and to march to encounter the earl of Leicester and his friends,
who were leading the king of England and his son to Hereford as
prisoners; who marched on, being accompanied by his own army
and that of the prince of North Wales, while Simon, his second son,
as the general and commander of the royal army, which had been
levied throughout the kingdom, advanced from the other side, so
that the two hemmed in the earls of Gloucester and Warrenne, and
the lords marchers, and slew them all. But by the overruling providence of God, who is the doorkeeper of prisons, the release of
the prisoners was effected, and on the Thursday in Whitsun week,
the eldest son of the king went out into the fields about Hereford
with his comrades and guards to take exercise, and then, when they
had all mounted their destrier horses, and fatigued them with gal-

loping, he, after that, mounted a horse of his own which was not
tired, and requesting leave of his companions (though he did not
obtain it), he went with all speed to the lord Roger de Mortimer,
at Wigemor. And the next day, the earls of Gloucester and Warrenne, with their followers, met Edward at Ludlow, and forgetting
all their mutual injuries and quarrels, and renewing their friendship, they proceeded with courage and alacrity to break down the
bridges and sink the ferry-boats over the Severn. Afterwards, as
their force was increased by the friends of the aforesaid Edward,
whom the power of the adverse party had long compelled to lie
hid, and when they had taken Gloucester, and treated the prisoners
with most extravagant cruelty, the earl of Leicester and his army,
being hemmed in the district about Hereford, were compelled to
lead their nominal king about as a prisoner, and to subject him,
against his will, to all the hardships of captivity.

And when Simon, the son of the aforesaid earl of Leicester, had,
with many barons and knights, traversed and plundered all Kent,
and the country about Winchester and the other southern districts
of England, and then proceeded, to his own misfortune, with great
speed to Kenilworth to meet his father, the aforesaid Edward and
Gilbert and their armies, being, by the favour of God, forewarned
of his approach, attacked his army at dawn on the day of Saint
Peter ad Vincula, and took them all prisoners, except Simon and
a few with him who escaped into the castle, and put them in chains,
and stripped those robbers and plunderers of all their booty, and
so celebrated a day of feasting at the New Chains.

The earl of Leicester and his companions, being ignorant of
this event, and marching on with all speed, reached the river Severn
that very same day, and having examined the proper fords, crossed
the river at twilight with the design of meeting and finding the
aforesaid Simon and his army, who were coming from England,
and having stopped the two next days on the borders of Worcester-
shire, on the third day they entered the town of Evesham, and
while they were occupying themselves there with refreshing their
souls, which had been long fainting under hunger and thirst, with
a little food, their scouts brought them word that the lord Edward
and his army were not above two miles off. So the earl of Leicester
and the barons marching out with their lord the king (whom they
took with them by force) to the rising ground of a gentle hill, beheld Edward and his army on the top of a hill, not above a stone's
throw from them, and hastening to them. And a wonderful conflict
took place, there being slain on the part of the lord Edward only

one knight of moderate prowess, and two esquires. On the other side there fell on the field of battle Simon, earl of Leicester, whose head, and hands, and feet were cut off, and Henry, his son, Hugh Despenser, justiciary of England, Peter de Montfort, William de Mandeville, Radulph Basset, Roger St. John, Walter de Despigny, William of York, and Robert Tregos, all very powerful knights and barons, and besides all the guards and warlike cavalry fell in the battle, with the exception of ten or twelve nobles, who were taken prisoners. And the names of the nobles who were wounded and taken prisoners were as follows: Guy de Montfort, son of the earl of Leicester, John Fitz-John, Henry de Hastings, Humphrey de Bohun the younger, John de Vescy, Peter de Montfort the younger, and Nicholas de Segrave. . . .

Therefore, the battle of Evesham having been thus gallantly fought, the king and the nobles of the kingdom assembled at Winchester, and ordered that the richer citizens of the city of London should be thrust into prison, that the citizens should be deprived of their ancient liberties, and that the palisades and chains with which the city was fortified should be removed, because the citizens had boldly adhered to Simon de Montfort, earl of Leicester, in contempt of the king and also to the injury of the kingdom; all which was done, for the more powerful citizens were thrown into prison at the castle of Windsor, and were afterwards punished with a pecuniary fine of no inconsiderable amount. All liberty was forbidden to the citizens, and the Tower of London was made stronger by the palisades and chains which had belonged to the city.

After this, a sentence of confiscation was pronounced at Westminster, on the feast of the translation of the blessed Edward, against the king's enemies, whose lands the king bestowed without delay on his own faithful followers. But some of those against whom this sentence was pronounced redeemed their possessions by payment of a sum of money, others uniting in a body lay hid in the woods, living miserably on plunder and rapine; the most powerful and mischievous of whom was Robert, earl Ferrars, who was restored to the full possession of his property, on condition that if ever he departed from his loyalty to the king, he should lose his earldom. . . .

13. The Chronicler of Bury St. Edmunds: Edward I and the Scottish Crown

In these passages, written by an anonymous late thirteenth-century chronicler of the royal abbey of Bury St. Edmunds, one sees revealed the important role which abbeys played in the government of the High Middle Ages. One notes, for instance, that this chronicler, in telling of Edward I's intervention in Scottish affairs, which had tragic final results, quotes documents which were specifically sent to him from the royal court to be inserted in his chronicle. This is in much the same way that today a Senator's speech is inserted in *The Congressional Record* or quoted by *The New York Times*. One also finds that Edward I was consulting Scottish abbey chronicles to help discover the rights of the various claimants to the Scottish throne. To view the monastic life of this age, then, as a retreat from the world seems an error. Most of those who lived in the abbeys of the period and composed their chronicles might better be compared to the Harold Nicolsons or Theodore Sorensens of our own day, whose writings are part of that game of high politics which occupies those who exercise power and influence in government. [From *The Chronicle of Bury St. Edmunds*, ed. and trans. Antonia Grandsden (London: Thomas Nelson & Sons Ltd, 1964), pp. 96 and 98–103. Reprinted with the omission of footnotes by permission of the publisher.]

[In 1290] the death took place in the Orkney islands of Margaret, the daughter of Eric, king of Norway, and Margaret. The latter was the daughter of Alexander, king of Scotland (who had died previously without an heir of the body), and Queen Margaret, daughter of Henry III, king of England, and sister of King Edward, that king's son. To [Margaret, daughter of Eric] belonged the hereditary right to the throne of Scotland as the nearest to it in blood. It had been hoped that she would marry Edward, son of the aforesaid King Edward, and a dispensation had already been sought in the Roman court. Eleanor, queen of England, the king's consort, died at Harby in Lincolnshire on 28 November. She was buried at Westminster with a magnificent procession and great pomp on 17 December, [1290]. After this the king travelled to the earl of Cornwall's hermitage at Ashridge to keep Christmas.

*   *   *

[In 1291] as all the descendants and blood-relatives of Alexander, the late king of Scotland, were dead and the line extinct, certain men in Scotland undertook to claim their hereditary right to the throne. The king of England saw this and asserted that the over-lordship of the kingdom belonged to him. In order to establish his claim with more support, he went to Norham in the Marches of Scotland and summoned monks from some of the churches in England to come there with their chronicles. The chronicles were inspected, investigated and discussed before all the king's council; and it was clear to one and all that the overlordship of Scotland belonged and ought to belong to the king. When all this had been recited before the notables of Scotland, that is before the bishops, earls and others, and the evidence carefully weighed, since the Scots had nothing to say they accepted the king as overlord. They entrusted to him as their lord the castles of Scotland, both this side of the Scottish sea and beyond it, together with the seal of Scotland, and swore fealty to him. They gave security by letters patent and declared that those who had claimed the throne of Scotland should abide by the judgment of the king of England's court. Then John de Baliol, Robert de Bruce and the others listed below presented themselves to vindicate their claim. At length they agreed to submit to the judgment of forty lawful men of each kingdom for the one party, and likewise forty for the other party, and twenty men repre-senting the king of England, with the intention that after the arguments and claims of each individual had been put before them, they should pronounce and publish their decision on the morrow of the feast of St. Peter ad Vincula. When this was done the king of England made the bishop of Caithness chancellor of Scotland and appointed one of the clerks of the chancery of England called Walter de Amersham to help him, stipulating that everything was to be done with Walter's advice and consent. The king distributed the responsibility for the castles among his liege men as suited him. He also appointed keepers of the peace and of good order and others to carry out the king's business, to act on both sides of the Scottish sea. So on the morrow of St. Peter's day, as aforesaid, impor-tant men of both kingdoms and all those who had presented a claim to the throne of Scotland appeared before the king at Berwick. It was decided with common counsel that all the claims were invalid and of no weight except those of John de Baliol, Robert de Bruce, John de Hastings and the others named below. The morrow of the next Trinity Sunday was assigned to the parties for the hearing of their claims at Berwick in the presence of the king and some of his liege men, who were to meet him there. When this had been arranged Florence, count of Holland, Robert de Bruce, lord of Annandale, John de Baliol, lord of Galloway, John de Hastings, lord of Abergavenny, John Comyn, lord of Badenoch, Patrick de Dunbar, earl of the March, John de Vescy, on behalf of his father, Nicholas de Soules and William de Ross, in whom or in one of whom the right to the throne of Scotland was believed to rest, returned home to await the day fixed for the presentation and discussion of their claims to such right or rights. As the king considered that the gist of the monastic chronicles made his rights over the kingdom of Scotland perfectly clear and as he wished to put what he had done on permanent record for all time, he wrote in the following form to the most important religious houses in England: "Edward, by the grace of God, king of England, lord of Ireland and duke of Aquitaine, to the abbot and convent of Bury St. Edmunds, his beloved in Christ, greetings. We are sending you under the seal of our Exchequer appended to these presents copies of certain letters which are in our treasury; the contents are as follows: 'To those who see or hear this letter we, Florence, count of Holland, Robert de Bruce, lord of Annandale, John de Baliol, lord of Galloway, John de Hastings, lord of Abergavenny, John Comyn, lord of Badenoch, Patrick de Dunbar, earl of the March, John de Vescy, on behalf of his father, Nicholas de Soules and William de Ross, give greetings in the Lord. Because we believe that we have a right to the throne of Scotland and mean to show, justify and assert this right in front of him who has the greatest power, jurisdiction and right to hear our claims, and because the noble Prince Edward, by the grace of God king of England, has informed us with good and adequate arguments that the supreme overlordship of Scotland belongs to him, together with responsibility for the kingdom and the right of hearing, trying and deciding the right of our claims, we of our own free will, without being forced or in any way compelled, wish and undertake to accept judgment of our case from him as overlord of the land. And we wish and promise to ratify and uphold his decision and that the kingdom of Scotland shall be handed to him for whom judgment is given in the king's presence. In witness of these things we have put our seals to this letter, made and given at Norham on the Tuesday after Ascension day in the year of grace 1291.' 'To all those who see or hear this letter we, Florence, count of Holland, Robert de Bruce, lord of Annandale, John de Baliol, lord of Galloway, John de Hastings, lord of Abergavenny, John Comyn, lord of Badenoch, Patrick de

Dunbar, earl of the March, John de Vescy, on behalf of his father, Nicholas de Soules and William de Ross, give greetings in the Lord. Since we of our own free will and common assent, without any coercion, have granted and conceded to the noble Prince Edward, by the grace of God king of England, that he as overlord of the land of Scotland may hear, try and decide our claims and demands, which we mean to show and assert, concerning our right to the throne of Scotland, and to accept judgment before him as overlord of the land, and have promised to uphold his action and that the kingdom shall be handed to him for whom judgment is given in the king's presence, but as the king of England cannot hold this sort of responsibility without the power of judgment, nor judgment nor right without the power of execution, and he can have no power of execution without the possession and seisin of the land itself and its castles, we wish, concede and grant that he, as overlord responsible for carrying out the above-mentioned duties, should have seisin of all the land and castles of Scotland. In order, however, that justice be done to the claimants, he should, before he has seisin as aforesaid, give good and sufficient security to the claimants, guardians and whole community of the realm of Scotland to return the same kingdom and castles with all the royal power, dignity, lordship, franchises, customary liberties, privileges, laws, customs, possessions and everything belonging to the kingdom, in the same condition as they were when seisin was entrusted to him. He should also deliver the realm to him in whose favour the law of the kingdom by royal judgment should decide, saving the right of the king of England to the homage of him who will be king. The kingdom should be returned within two months after the day when the lawful claim is investigated and affirmed. In the meantime the revenues of the land should be safely deposited and carefully kept by the chamberlain of Scotland, whoever he is, and by he who shall be assigned to the chamberlain by the king of England, under their seals, except only a reasonable sum to be spent for the maintenance of the land, castles and the officials of the kingdom. In witness of these things we have put our seals to this letter. Made and given at Norham on Wednesday after Ascension day, in the year of grace 1291.' We command you, therefore, that you have these letters recorded in your chronicles so that these events are remembered forever. Witnessed by Master William de March, our treasurer, at Westminster on 9 July in the nineteenth year of our reign by writ under the privy seal." . . .

Part Four

❧ ITALY

14. John of Salisbury: Arnold of Brescia and Papal Rome

John of Salisbury, who died about 1180, was probably the greatest humanist of the twelfth century. His career illustrates the international character of medieval scholarship during this period. Although he was born an Englishman, he taught for many years in the cathedral school of Chartres (France) and ended his life as bishop there. He also found time during these years to serve in the papal court in Italy. Though he is best known as the author of a famous book on statecraft, called the *Policraticus*, his writings are represented here by a selection from his *Memoirs of the Papal Court*. In it he gives us a picture of Arnold of Brescia, a reformer and pupil of Abélard, who, until his expulsion and execution in 1155 by the Emperor Frederick I Barbarossa (1152–1190), led a rebellion against the papacy and became chief of a Roman communal republic. There is also a description of the alliance which united the ruthless and powerful King Roger II of Sicily (1101–1154) with the papacy, which needed his support to oppose the German Emperor and local Roman opponents alike. [From *Memoirs of the Papal Court* by John of Salisbury, trans. Marjorie Chibnall (London: Thomas Nelson & Sons Ltd., 1956), pp. 62–67. Reprinted with the omission of footnotes by permission of the publisher.]

Negotiations for peace were proceeding between the pope and the Romans, and numerous legations sped to and fro between the two parties. But there were many obstacles in the way of peace, the greatest of all being the refusal of the Romans to expel Arnold of Brescia, who was said to have bound himself by oath to uphold the honour of the city and Roman republic. The Romans in their turn promised him aid and counsel against all men, and explicitly against the lord pope; for the Roman church had excommunicated him and ordered him to be shunned as a heretic. This man was a priest by office, a canon regular by profession, and one who had mortified his flesh with fasting and coarse raiment: of keen intelligence, persevering in his study of the scriptures, eloquent in speech, and a vehement preacher against the vanities of the world. Nevertheless he was reputed to be factious and a leader of schism, who wherever he lived prevented the citizens from being at peace with the clergy. He had been abbot of Brescia, and when the bishop was absent on a short visit to Rome had so swayed the minds of the citizens that they would scarcely open their gates to the bishop on his return. For this he was deposed by Pope Innocent [1] and expelled from Italy; crossing the Alps into France he became a disciple of Peter Abailard, and together with Master Hyacinth, who is now a cardinal, zealously fostered his cause against the abbot of Clairvaux.[2] After Master Peter had set out for Cluny, he remained at Paris on the Mont Sainte Geneviève, expounding the scriptures to scholars at the church of St. Hilary where Peter had been lodged. But he had no listeners except poor students who publicly begged their bread from door to door to support themselves and their master. He said things that were entirely consistent with the law accepted by Christian people, but not at all with the life they led. To the bishops he was merciless on account of their avarice and filthy lucre; most of all because of stains on their personal lives, and their striving to build the church of God in blood. He denounced the abbot, whose name is renowned above all others for his many virtues, as a seeker after vainglory, envious of all who won distinction in learning or religion unless they were his own disciples. In consequence the abbot prevailed on the most Christian king to expel him from the Frankish kingdom; from there he returned to Italy after Pope Innocent's death and, after promising reparation and obedience to the Roman church, was received at Viterbo by Pope Eugenius.[3] Penance was imposed on him, which he claimed to have performed in fasts, vigils and prayers in the holy

---

[1] [Pope Innocent II was a special protégé of St. Bernard who, thanks to the latter, was finally recognized as pope by all Europe—ED.]

[2] [This refers to St. Bernard (1090–1153), who was the leading churchman of the period and who opposed Abélard's philosophical ideas and had them condemned—ED.]

[3] [The new pope who succeeded Pope Innocent II—ED.]

places of the city; and again he took a solemn oath to show obedience. Whilst dwelling in Rome under pretext of penance he won
the city to his side, and preaching all the more freely because the
lord pope was occupied in Gaul he built up a faction known as the
heretical sect of the Lombards. He had disciples who imitated his
austerities and won favour with the populace through outward
decency and austerity of life, but found their chief supporters
amongst pious women, He himself was frequently heard on the
Capitol and in public gatherings. He had already publicly denounced the cardinals, saying that their college, by its pride, avarice,
hypocrisy and manifold shame was not the church of God, but a
place of business and den of thieves, which took the place of the
scribes and Pharisees amongst Christian peoples. The pope himself
was not what he professed to be—an apostolic man and shepherd
of souls—but a man of blood who maintained his authority by fire
and sword, a tormentor of churches and oppressor of the innocent,
who did nothing in the world save gratify his lust and empty other
men's coffers to fill his own. He was, he said, so far from apostolic
that he imitated neither the life nor the doctrine of the apostles,
wherefore neither obedience nor reverence was due to him: and in
any case no man could be admitted who wished to impose a yoke
of servitude on Rome, the seat of Empire, fountain of liberty and
mistress of the world.

Since the tumults of the Romans were unbearable to the pope,
he took the road for Anagni, to treat for peace by ambassadors with
the king of Sicily. For the king, after the fashion of tyrants, had
reduced the church in his kingdom to slavery, and instead of allow-
ing any freedom of election named in advance the candidate to be
elected, so disposing of all ecclesiastical offices like palace appoint-
ments. Consequently the Roman church had forbidden the consecration of men elected in this way, and the prohibition had gone
to such lengths that few sees were blessed with bishops of their
own, and men who had been elected years before, but never consecrated, resided in almost every cathedral church. For the country
had been deprived of consecrated oil, as a penalty for the capture
of Pope Innocent II. As an added injury, the king would suffer no
papal legate to enter his territory, except at his summons or with
his express permission, and these were not supported by the
churches independently, but either out of his own revenues or by
the churches at his command. It is true that in making appoint-
ments to churches he was held guiltless of open simony, and took

pride in presenting decent men wherever they might be found. If he came across any bishop who was proscribed or exiled he gladly aided him, and all foreigners were more or less welcome in his domain, except men of the kingdom of Germany, whom he was unwilling to have among his subjects; for he distrusted that people and could not endure their barbarous ways. Those elected to churches with the king's cognisance offered obedience and reverence to the papacy; but not one of them could secure consecration. So the king sought for a conference with the lord pope, and flinging himself at his feet near Ceprano on the boundary between their dominions agreed to grant free elections to churches and allow the pope to examine elections already made, approving or rejecting them as he thought fit; he also granted him free disposal of the churches, as he or his legates on his behalf should ordain. Then he besought the pope to accept his homage and renew his privileges, but neither his prayers nor his gifts were of any avail. When peace had been made in this way between the church and the king, they parted friends: the king offered devoted service to the pope and curia, and placing his lands at their disposal promised that in future he would faithfully minister to the needs of the papacy. Most of the elect were consecrated, the remainder rejected as the lord pope thought proper; but none were subjected to such a searching examination, and none so lightly rejected that it became common knowledge in the church. The electors swore repeatedly that they had not been influenced in their choice by the king's mandate or nomination, directly or indirectly. The life, learning, status and birth of the elect were discussed; and the pope refused to take anything from those who were accepted for consecration, or knowingly to permit others to take anything, both for reasons of conscience and to avoid scandal; for he was afraid of giving the crafty king of Sicily, who perpetually tried to catch the church in some fault, any plausible grounds for accusation. . . .

15. Otto of Freising: Frederick Barbarossa's First Intervention in Northern Italy

Bishop Otto of Freising (1110–1158) was the uncle of the Emperor Frederick Barbarossa and one of the more profound historians of the Middle Ages. He is perhaps best known for his book entitled *The Two Cities*, in which he displays a special Christian view of the historical process. The selection chosen here, however, is of a rather different character. It is from a book describing the early years of the reign of the Emperor Frederick of which Otto wrote only the first two books, the remainder of them being completed by his less-talented continuator, Rahewin.

What is of particular interest in this selection of Otto's work is his description of the city of Milan, especially its social classes and political ambitions—a very perceptive contemporary account of an Italian city-state. Upon reading it one should be able to understand why Frederick clashed with Milan in such a way that eventually, twenty years later, at the Battle of Legnano (1177), he met a disastrous defeat. One can also see here how Italian communes were the incubators of the very different civic world of the later Italian Renaissance. [From *The Deeds of Frederick Barbarossa* by Otto of Freising, trans. Charles C. Mierow (New York: Columbia University Press: 1953), pp. 127–34. Copyright © 1953 by Columbia University Press. Reprinted with the omission of footnotes by permission of the publisher.]

[Italy] began to be subject to the invasions and the domination of the barbarians who, coming from the island of Scandza [Scandinavia] with their leader Alboin, first inhabited the Pannonias, from them it began to be called Lombardy. For to increase their army [by the drafting of women] they twisted the womens' hair about the chin in such a way as to imitate a manly and bearded face, and for that reason they were called Lombards (*Longobardi*), from their long beards. Hence it came to pass that as the ancient inhabitants of that province were crowded together around the exarchate of Ravenna, that part of Italy (which was formerly called Aemilia) is commonly called even today *Romaniola*, which is known to be a diminutive, derived from "Rome."

But [the Lombards] having put aside crude, barbarious ferocity, perhaps from the fact that when united in marriage with the natives they begat sons who inherited something of the Roman gentleness and keenness from their mothers' blood, and from the very quality of the country and climate, retain the refinement of the Latin speech and their elegance of manners. In the governing of their cities, also, and in the conduct of public affairs, they still imitate the wisdom of the ancient Romans. Finally, they are so desirous of liberty that, avoiding the insolence of power, they are governed by the will of consuls rather than rulers. There are known to be three orders among them: captains, vavasors, and commoners. And in order to suppress arrogance, the aforesaid consuls are chosen not from one but from each of the classes. And lest they should exceed bounds by lust for power, they are changed almost every year. The consequence is that, as practically that entire land is divided among the cities, each of them requires its bishops to live in the cities, and scarcely any noble or great man can be found in all the surrounding territory who does not acknowledge the authority of his city. And from this power to force all elements together they are wont to call the several lands of each [noble, or magnate] their contado. Also, that they may not lack the means of subduing their neighbors, they do not disdain to give the girdle of knighthood or the grades of distinction to young men of inferior station and even some workers of the vile mechanical arts, whom other peoples bar like the pest from the more respected and honorable pursuits. From this it has resulted that they far surpass all other states of the world in riches and in power. They are aided in this not only, as has been said, by their characteristic industry, but also by the absence of their princes, who are accustomed to remain on the far side of the Alps. In this, however, forgetful of their ancient nobility, they retain traces of their barbaric imperfection, because while boasting that they live in accordance with law, they are not obedient to the laws. For they scarcely if ever respect the prince to whom they should display the voluntary deference of obedience or willingly perform that which they have sworn by the integrity of their laws, unless they sense his authority in the power of his great army. Therefore it often happens that although a citizen must be humbled by the laws and an adversary subdued by arms in accordance with the laws, yet they very frequently receive in hostile fashion him whom they ought to accept as their own gentle prince, when he demands what is rightfully his own. From this arises a twofold loss to the common weal: the prince is obliged to assemble an army for the subjugation of his people, and the people (not without great loss of their own possessions) are forced to obey their prince. Accordingly, by the same process of reasoning whereby impetuosity accuses the people for this situation, so should necessity excuse the prince in the sight of God and men.

Among all the cities of this people Milan now holds chief place. It is situated between the Po and the Pyrenees, and between the Ticino and the Adda, which take their source from the same Pyrenees and drain into the Po, thereby creating a certain very fertile valley, like an island. Located midway, it is rightly called *Mediolanum*, although some think it was named *Mediolanum* by its founders from a certain portentous sow that had bristles on one side and wool on the other. Now this city is considered (as has been said) more famous than others not only because of its size and its abundance of brave men, but also from the fact that it has extended its authority over two neighboring cities situated within the same valley, Como and Lodi. Furthermore—as usually happens in our transitory lot when favoring fortune smiles—Milan, elated by prosperity, became puffed up to such audacious exaltation that not only did it not shrink from molesting its neighbors, but recently even dared incur the anger of the prince, standing in no awe of his majesty. From what causes this situation arose I shall afterward briefly set forth.

Meanwhile, it seems necessary to say a few words concerning the jurisdiction over the realm. For it is an old custom, maintained from the time that the Roman empire passed over to the Franks even down to our own day, that as often as the kings have decided to enter Italy they send ahead certain qualified men of their retinue to go about among the individual cities and towns to demand what pertains to the royal treasury and is called by the natives *fodrum*. Hence it comes about that, on the prince's arrival, most of the cities, towns, and strongholds that attempt to oppose this right by absolute refusal or by not making full payment are razed to the ground to give evidence of their impudence to posterity. Likewise, another right is said to have found its source in ancient custom. When the prince enters Italy all dignities and magistracies must be vacated and everything administered by his nod, in accordance with legal decrees and the judgment of those versed in the law. The judges are said also to accord him so great authority over the land that they think it just to supply for the use of the king as much as he needs from all that the land customarily produces that is essential for his use and may be of advantage to the army, only excepting the cattle and the seed devoted to the cultivation of the soil.

Now the king abode, it is said, for five days [November 30–December 6, 1154] at Roncaglia and held a diet, with the princes, consuls, and elders of almost all the cities assembled there, and diverse things became known from the complaints of this party or of that. Among them were William, marchese of Montferrat, a noble and great man, and practically the only one of the barons of Italy who could escape from the authority of the cities, and also the bishop of Asti. They made serious charges: one, concerning the insolence of the people of Asti; the other (that is, the marchese), concerning that of the inhabitants of Chieri.

(But we do not think that, in comparison with his other valiant exploits, it contributes much to the prince's claim to glory if, while hastening on to more important things, we speak of the fortified places, rocky strongholds, towns, and great estates destroyed since his coming, not only by those of knightly order but even by the assault of the unbridled sergeants.)

There were present also the consuls of Como and of Lodi, making mournful lament over the arrogance of the people of Milan. They bewailed their long-continued misery of mistreatment in the presence of two consuls of that very city, Oberto de Orto and Gerardo Negri. Therefore, as the prince was about to visit the upper regions of Italy and wished to pass through the Milanese territory he kept the aforesaid consuls with him to guide his way and to make arrangements for suitable places for encampments.

There came also to the same court ambassadors of the people of Genoa, who not long before this time had captured Almeria and Lisbon,[1] renowned cities in Spain, very famous for their workmanship of silk cloths, and returned laden with spoils of the Saracens. They presented the prince with lions, ostriches, parrots, and other valuable gifts.

Frederick, therefore, being (as has been said) about to set out for the upper regions of Farther Italy, led his forces from Roncaglia and pitched camp in the territory of the Milanese. And as he was conducted by the aforesaid consuls through wastelands where provisions (*stipendia*) could neither be found nor secured by purchase, he was moved to anger and turned his arms against the people of Milan, having first ordered the consuls to return home. Another circumstance aggravated his wrath. The whole army is said to have been so exasperated by a heavy downpour of rain that in consequence of this double annoyance—hunger and the inclement

[1] [This is an error. Lisbon was captured by a northern European expedition. See selection 24—Ed.]

weather—all aroused the prince against the consuls as much as they could. There was likewise another by no means trivial cause for this high feeling. The prince had already perceived their swollen insolence in the fact that they were not only unwilling to rebuild the cities which they had destroyed, but were even trying to bribe and to corrupt his noble and hitherto untarnished spirit to acquiesce in their iniquity. The king, moving his camp from the barren region, betook himself to fertile places of this land, not far from the city, and refreshed his weary soldiers.

There was in the vicinity a certain fairly well-populated town, Rosate, where the people of Milan had stationed a garrison of about five hundred armed knights. These knights were then ordered to return to the city, and all that was useful having been taken as plunder, the town itself was given up to the flames. Thereupon certain of the knights of the prince, advancing to the gates of the Milanese, wounded some and took others captive. The people of Milan, not only aghast at their present loss but also in fear for the future, in order to assuage the anger of the prince destroyed the house of the consul, Gerardo, as the author of this calamity. But the prince, taking no thought of this incident, proceeded to the Ticino River to bring greater disasters upon them. This river, rising (as has been shown above) from the Pyrenees and emptying into the Po, or *Eridanus,* near Pavia (which for this reason is called *Ticinus*), encompasses the island of the Milanese on the western side. There he seized two wooden bridges, which they had built for an attack on the people of Pavia and of Novara, and had fortified with bulwarks to check their assault. After sending his army over them, he gave them up to the flames.

Then he captured and burned three of the fortified and excellent strongholds, namely, Momo, Galliate, and Trecate, which they had established in the territory of the people of Novara for their subjugation. Now Novara is not a large city, but since its reconstruction (after it was in times past destroyed by Emperor Henry)[2] it has been fortified with a new wall and a good-sized rampart. It has within its diocese Count Guido of Biandrate, who contrary to Italian custom rules all the territory of this city, scarcely excepting the city itself, by authority of the people of Milan—these as yet insatiable Milanese, who had heretofore desired to absorb both this city and Pavia, as they had the cities before mentioned. This victory was won in the month of December, and the Lord's birthday was

[2] [By Henry V in 1110—ED.]

celebrated by the prince with great rejoicing over the destruction of the aforesaid strongholds.

After this [1155] the prince, proceeding through Vercelli and Turin, crossed the Po there and directed his march to the lowlands, toward Pavia. But the townsmen of Chieri as well as the citizens of Asti, because they had not obeyed the command of the prince that they do justice to William, marchese of Montferrat, were proscribed as enemies convicted of rebellion. When the king led his army to punish their disobedience, they forsook their fortifications as though distrusting their strength, and fled to the neighboring mountains. The king, coming first to Chieri and finding sufficient supplies, remained there for several days. He destroyed the towers that were there—not a few—and burned the town. Then proceeding to Asti and finding it empty, not of resources but of inhabitants, he stayed there for several days and gave it up to fire and pillage. But before he moved his camp from there, the king took counsel with men of prudence and decided to enact some regulations advantageous to the soldiers in the future, on account of the frequent dissensions that had broken out in the army. He issued an order, not merely by public announcement but also through the administering of an oath to everyone of high and low degree, that none should venture to carry a sword within the confines of the camp to the possible hurt of a fellow soldier. He added as a penalty that whosoever wounded any of his fellows in violation of this peace regulation (*treugam*) should lose a hand or even have his head cut off. After this order—as wise as it was necessary—had been laid down, the thoughtless violence of youthful spirits was calmed.

Not far from that place there was a city named Tortona, fortified by nature and art, friendly to the people of Milan and allied by treaty with them against the people of Pavia. Accordingly, as the people of Pavia complained that they were troubled more by Tortona than by Milan (for although the city of Pavia is, indeed, situated in the valley of the people of Milan, the chief extent of its territory is on the other side of the Ticino River, exposed to Tortona with no intervening mountain or stream), Tortona was ordered by the prince to withdraw from its alliance with Milan and to associate with Pavia. When it refused to do this, it too was proscribed as guilty of treason and numbered among the enemies of the empire, because it had chosen to cling rather to a seditious and hostile city than to one that was peaceful and loyal to the kings. The prince, in order to punish the insolence of the people of Tortona in like

fashion to that of the inhabitants of Asti, moved his camp from
Asti and pitched his tents at a certain town which is called Bosco.
After delaying there for several days, he decided to send ahead
certain of the knights in company with his brother Conrad, Berthold,
duke of the Burgundians, and his standard-bearer Otto, the count
palatine of Bavaria, to investigate the situation of the city. They
crossed the river [Scrivia], hastened down to the city itself, and
after inspecting everything pitched camp not far from it on the
aforesaid stream. On the third day after this, the king followed his
men and fixed his tents on the opposite bank of the stream, being
unable to join his companions because of the flooding of the aforesaid river, which had increased to more than its usual size from a
sudden downpour of rain. Nevertheless, not long afterward, when
the little stream had somewhat subsided, he joined his men by
managing to wade across, and hastened to the city. At the first
assault he stormed and took the suburbs, defended by a wall and
towers. The citizens scarcely had an opportunity to retreat to the
citadel under cover of the night which was now coming on and a
storm that was rising. Now Tortona is almost at the foot of the
Apennine mountains, being located at the point where the Apen-
nines and the Pyrenees are united, as has been said before, and
looks out upon the plain of Pavia and Milan as from a watchtower.
Placed on a smooth mountain whose rocky face projects over its
precipitous sides, it glories in its towers. One in particular, of brick,
was built long ago by Tarquin the Proud and is now called *Rubea*.
Tortona is notable for a suburb on the steep mountainside and
gains distinction from the circuit of its walls and the number of
its lofty towers and of its people, and for a certain little rivulet
[Ossona] that flows through its midst.

The prince having taken the suburb (as has been said) laid siege
to the citadel, or the city itself. But this citadel had been garrisoned
for defense not only by its own troops, but also by the forces of
the Milanese and of the neighboring barons (one of whom was the
marchese Obizzo, surnamed Malaspina). Made confident by so much
support, Tortona dared to prepare to ward off the anger of the
prince. . . . [Tortona survived its siege—ED.]

16. Bonaventura: The Early Life of St. Francis

This life of St. Francis of Assisi, which was written by Bonaventura shortly after the former's death, reveals a very different facet of Italian town life than that shown in Otto of Freising's description of Milan. Francis was a bourgeois and had a merchant father devoted to business and profit, but his saintly biographer makes it clear that he was anything but devoted to the values of the market place. Even before his conversion he was much attracted to knightly and chivalric ideals, and he maintained a romantic approach to life until the end of his days. In reading this over religious and somehow conventional description of St. Francis, then, we should be able to see a man who transcended his middle-class background and, in the Franciscan movement, created a great force for the spiritual rebirth of Europe. The life of this orthodox reforming successor of Arnold of Brescia serves to remind us that the Italian urban scene in the course of the twelfth and thirteenth centuries was a remarkably varied one. [From *The Life of St. Francis* by Bonaventura, in *The Little Flowers of St. Francis,* trans. Thomas Okey (New York: E. P. Dutton & Co., Inc., 1910) [Everyman's Library Edition], pp. 307-9, 316, and 319-21. Reprinted by permission of the publisher.

There was a man in the city of Assisi, by name Francis, whose memory is blessed. . . . For, albeit in his youth he was reared in vanity amid the vain sons of men, and, after gaining some knowledge of letters, was appointed unto a profitable business of merchandise, nevertheless, by the aid of the divine protection, he went not astray among the wanton youth after the lusts of the flesh, albeit given up unto pleasures; nor among the covetous merchants, albeit intent on his gains, did he put his trust in money and treasure. For there was divinely implanted in the heart of the young Francis a certain generous compassion toward the poor, the which, growing up with him from infancy, had so filled his heart with kindliness that, when he came to be no deaf hearer of the Gospel, he was minded to give unto all that asked of him, in especial if they pleaded the love of God.

*　　　　　*　　　　　*

But as yet Francis knew not the intent of God concerning him, forasmuch as he was both drawn away unto external things by his father's calling, and weighed down toward earthly things by the corruption inborn in our nature, and had not yet learned to contemplate heavenly things, nor accustomed himself to taste of divine. And, because the infliction of tribulation giveth understanding unto the spirit, the hand of the Lord was upon him and the changes of the right hand of the Most High, afflicting his body with protracted sickness, that so He might prepare his soul for the anointing of the Holy Spirit. Now when he had regained his bodily strength, and had made ready for himself in his wonted fashion meet apparel, he met a certain soldier, of noble birth, but poor and ill-clad; whereupon, compassionating his poverty, with a kindly impulse he forthwith did off his garments and put them on him, thus in one act fulfilling a two-fold ministry of kindliness, insomuch as he both covered the shame of a noble knight, and relieved the destitution of a poor man.

Now on the night following, when he had yielded himself unto sleep, the divine mercy showed him a fair and great palace, together with military accoutrements adorned with the sign of the Cross of Christ, thus setting forth unto him that the mercy he had shown unto the poor soldier for the love of the King Most High was to be recompensed by this peerless reward. Accordingly, when he enquired whose were these things, answer was made him by a divine declaration that they all were his own and his soldiers'. Then, waking at early morn—since he had not yet practised his mind in examining the divine mysteries, and knew not how to pass through the appearance of things seen unto the beholding of the truth of things unseen he accounted this strange vision a token of great good fortune. Wherefore he purposed, being as yet ignorant of the divine counsel, to betake himself into Apulia, unto a certain munificent Count, hoping in his service to win glory in arms, as the vision shown unto him had betokened. With but little delay, he set forth on his journey and had gone as far as the neighbouring city; there he heard the Lord speaking unto him by night as with the voice of a friend, and saying, "Francis, who can do better for thee, the lord or the servant, the rich man or the poor?" And when Francis had made reply that alike the lord and the rich man could do the best, the Voice answered forthwith, "Why, then, dost thou leave the Lord for the servant, the rich God for a poor mortal?" And Francis said, "Lord, what wilt Thou have me to do?" And the Lord said unto him, "Return unto thy country, for the vision that thou hast seen betokeneth that which shall be spiritually wrought, and is to be fulfilled in thee not by mortal counsel, but by divine." So, when it was morning, he returned in haste toward Assisi, confident and rejoicing, awaiting the will of the Lord.

*   *   *

But when the townsfolk beheld him unkempt in appearance, and changed in mind, and on this account deemed him to have lost his senses, they rushed upon him with mud of the streets and stones, and mocked him with loud shouts as a fool and madman. . . . When his father heard these outcries, he ran out at once, not to deliver him, but rather to destroy him; laying aside all compunction, he dragged him into the house, and there afflicted him first with words, then with stripes and bonds. . . .
After a little space, on his father's departure from the country, his mother—who misliked her husband's dealings, and deemed it hopeless to soften the unyielding constancy of her son—freed him from his bonds, and let him go forth. Then he, giving thanks unto the Lord Almighty, returned unto the place where he had been afore. When his father returned, and found him not in the house, heaping reproaches on his wife, he ran in fury unto that place, intending, if he could not bring him back, at least to drive him from the province. But Francis, strengthened of God, of his own accord came forth to meet his raging father, crying aloud that he cared naught for his bonds and stripes, yea more, protesting that he would gladly endure all hardships for the sake of Christ. . . .
Then this father according unto the flesh was fain to take this son of grace, now stripped of his wealth, before the Bishop of the city, that into his hands he might resign his claim unto his father's inheritance, and render up all that had been his. This that true lover of poverty showed himself right ready to do, and coming into the Bishop's presence, he brooked no delays, he was kept back of none, tarried for no speech, nor spake himself, but at once did off all his garments, and restored them unto his father. . . . The Bishop, seeing this, and marvelling at such exceeding fervour in the man of God, rose forthwith, and, weeping, put his arms round him; then, devout and kindly man as he was, covered him with the cloak wherewith he himself was clad, bidding his servants give him something to clothe his limbs withal, and there was brought unto him a mean and rough tunic of a farm-servant of the Bishop.

*   *   *

Francis, now stablished in the humility of Christ, recalled unto
mind the obedience laid upon him by the Crucifix as to the re-
pairing of the church of Saint Damian, and like one truly obedient
returned unto Assisi, that he might, if even by begging, obtain means
to accomplish the divine behest. Laying aside all shamefastness for
the love of the Poor Man Crucified, he went about begging from
those who had known him in his affluence, bearing the loads of
stones on his frail body, worn with fasting. When the church
aforesaid had been repaired, the Lord helping him, and the devotion of the citizens coming unto his aid—that his body after its
toil might not relax in sloth, he turned to repair the church of
Saint Peter, at some distance from the city, by reason of the especial
devotion that in the purity of his candid faith he had for the Prince
of the Apostles.

*   *   *

On a day he was devoutly hearing the Mass of the Apostles, that
Gospel was read aloud wherein Christ gave unto His disciples that
were sent forth to preach the Gospel pattern for their life, to wit,
that they should possess neither gold, nor silver, nor money in
their purses, nor scrip for their journey, neither two coats, neither
shoes, nor yet staves. Hearing this, and understanding it, and committing it unto memory, the lover of Apostolic poverty was at once
filled with joy unspeakable. "This," saith he, "is what I desire, yea,
this what I long for with my whole heart." Forthwith he loosed his
shoes from off his feet, laid down his staff, cast aside his purse and
his money, contented him with one scanty tunic, and, throwing aside
his belt, took a rope for girdle, applying all the care of his heart
to discover how best he might fulfil that which he had heard,
and conform himself in all things unto the rule of Apostolic godli-
ness.

From this time forward, the man of God began, by divine impulse, to become a jealous imitator of Gospel poverty, and to invite
others unto penitence.

*   *   *

Now when the servant of Christ perceived that the number of
the Brethren was gradually increasing, he wrote for himself and
for his Brethren a Rule for their life, in simple words. Herein the
observance of the Holy Gospel was set as the inseparable foundation,

and some few other points were added that seemed necessary for a consistent manner of life. But he was fain that what he had written should be approved by the Supreme Pontiff, wherefore he purposed to approach the Apostolic See with that his company of simple men, relying only on the divine guidance. . . .

Now when he had come unto the Roman Curia, and had been introduced into the presence of the Supreme Pontiff, he expounded unto him his intent, humbly and earnestly beseeching him to sanction the Rule aforesaid for their life. And the Vicar of Christ, the lord Innocent the Third, a man exceeding renowned for wisdom, beholding in the man of God the wondrous purity of a simple soul, constancy unto his purpose, and the enkindled fervour of a holy will, was disposed to give unto the suppliant his fatherly sanction. Howbeit, he delayed to perform that which the little poor one of Christ asked, by reason that unto some of the Cardinals this seemed a thing untried, and too hard for human strength. But there was present among the Cardinals an honour-worthy man, the lord John of Saint Paul, Bishop of Sabina, a lover of all holiness, and an helper of the poor men of Christ. He, inflamed by the Divine Spirit, said unto the Supreme Pontiff, and unto his colleagues, "If we refuse the request of this poor man as a thing too hard, and untried, when his petition is that the pattern of Gospel life may be sanctioned for him, let us beware lest we stumble at the Gospel of Christ. For if any man saith that in the observance of Gospel perfection, and the vowing thereof there is contained aught that is untried, or contrary unto reason, or impossible to observe, he is clearly seen to blaspheme against Christ, the author of the Gospel." When these arguments had been set forth, the successor of the Apostle Peter turning unto the poor man of Christ, said, "Pray unto Christ my son, that He may show us His will through thee, and when we know it more surely, we will more confidently assent unto thy holy desires." . . . Then and there he granted his request, and promised at a later day to bestow yet more upon him. He sanctioned the Rule, and gave him a command to preach repentance, and made all the lay Brethren that had accompanied the servant of God wear narrow tonsures, that they might preach the word of God without hindrance.

17. Villani: Late Thirteenth-Century Florence

If one wishes to understand the political and economic life of a large Italian commune in the course of the thirteenth century, one cannot find a better guide than these selections of Giovanni Villani's *Chronicle*. Villani was just *one* of a group of town historians who emerged in late medieval Italy and who wrote to glorify their own particular city-state. But he was perhaps the most vivid of them all and the most penetrating in his understanding. In describing the Florence of Dante's day he manages to give us the feel of it—the disorders, the factions, the stalwart republicanism of its citizens and their economic accomplishments and aspirations. What may perhaps most amaze the modern reader is the constant strife that went on, the exile of losing factions, the building of private towers, and the political and family vendettas. The admirer of a peaceful, democratic existence will find Florence, as described by Villani, little to his taste. [From *Villani's Chronicle*, trans. Rose E. Selfe, ed. Philip H. Wickstead (London: Archibald Constable and Co., Ltd., 1906), pp. 309–15, 318–19, and 323–27. Reprinted by permission of the publisher.]

In the said year 1294, in the month of January, when Giovanni da Lucino da Como had lately entered upon the office of Podestà of Florence,[1] a cause for trial before him accusing Corso de' Donati, a noble and powerful citizen among the best in Florence, of having slain a popolano, a retainer of his associate Simone Galastrone, in a scuffle and fray which they had together, and wherein that retainer was slain; for which Corso Donati refused to pay the fine and bade justice take its course, trusting in a favour of the said Podestà, to be granted at the prayers of friends and of the lords; whereas the people of Florence looked that the said Podestà should condemn him; and already the standard of justice had been brought forth to carry the sentence into execution; but he absolved him; for the which thing, when the said declaration of innocence was read from the palace of the Podestà, and Simone Galastrone was condemned for having inflicted wounds, the common people

---

[1] [The Podestà was the chief magistrate of an Italian city-state—Ed.]

cried out: "Death to the Podestà," and sallied forth in haste from
the palace, crying, "To arms! to arms! long live the people!" and
a great number of the people flew to arms, and especially of the
common people, and rushed to the house of Giano della Bella,
their chief; and he, it is said, sent them with his brother to the
palace of the Priors[2] to follow the gonfalonier of justice; but this
they did not do, but came only to the palace of the Podestà, and
furiously assaulted the said palace with arms and crossbows, and
set fire to the gates and burnt them, and entered in, and seized
and scornfully robbed the said Podestà and his staff. But Corso in
fear of his life fled from the palace over the roofs, for then was it
not so walled as it is now. And the tumult displeased the Priors
which were very near to the palace of the Podestà, but by reason
of the unbridled populace, they were not able to hinder it. But
some days after, when the uproar had been quieted, the great men
could not rest, in their desire to abase Giano della Bella, forasmuch
as he had been among the chiefs and beginners of the Ordinances
of Justice, and was moreover desirous further to abase the magnates
by taking from the Captains of the Guelf Party the seal and the
common fund of the Party (which fund was very great), and to give
them to the commonwealth; not that he was not a Guelf and of
Guelf stock, but he would fain diminish the power of the magnates.
Wherefore the magnates, seeing themselves thus treated, created
a faction together with the Council of the College of Judges and
of Notaries, which held themselves to be oppressed by him, as we
before made mention, and with other popolani grassi, friends and
kinsmen of the magnates, which loved not that Giano della Bella
should be greater in the commonwealth than they. And they determined to elect a body of stalwart Priors. And this was done, and
they were proclaimed earlier than the wonted time. And this done,
when they were in office they conferred with the Captain of the
People, and set forth a proclamation and inquisition against the
said Giano della Bella and his other confederates and followers
and those which had been leaders in setting fire to the gates of the
Palace, charging them with having set the city in an uproar, and
disturbed the peace of the State, and assaulted the Podestà, against
the Ordinances of Justice; for the which thing the common people
was much disturbed, and went to the house of Giano della Bella,
and offered to surround him with arms, to defend him or to attack
the city. And his brother bore to Orto San Michele a standard with

[2] [The Priors were a board of town representatives of the Florentines during
these years—a kind of city council—Ed.]

the arms of the people; but Giano was a wise man, albeit somewhat presumptuous, and when he saw himself betrayed and deceived by the very men which had been with him in making the Popolo, and saw that their force together with that of the magnates was very great, and that the Priors were already assembled under arms at their house, he would not hazard the chances of civil war; and to the end the city might not be ravaged, and for fear of his person, he would not face the court, but withdrew, and departed from Florence on the fifth day of March, hoping that the people might yet restore him to his state; wherefore by the said accusation or notification he was for contumacy condemned in person and banished, and he died in exile in France (for he had affairs to attend to there, and was a partner of the Pazzi); and all his goods were destroyed; and certain other popolani were accused with him; and he was a great loss to our city, and above all to the people, forasmuch as he was the most leal and upright popolano, and lover of the common good, of any man in Florence, and one who gave to the commonwealth and took nothing therefrom. He was presumptuous and desired to avenge his wrongs, and this he did somewhat against the Abati, his neighbours, with the arm of the commonwealth, and, perhaps for the said sins, he was by his own laws, wrongfully and without guilt, judged by the unjust. And note that this is a great example to those citizens which are to come, to beware of desiring to be lords over their fellow-citizens or too ambitious; but to be content with the common citizenship. For the very men which had aided him to rise, through envy betrayed him and plotted to abase him; and it has been seen and experienced truly in Florence in ancient and modern times, that whosoever has become leader of the people and of the masses has been cast down; forasmuch as the ungrateful people never give men their due reward. From this event arose great disturbance and change amongst the people and in the city of Florence, and from that time forward the artificers and common people possessed little power in the commonwealth, but the government remained in the hands of the powerful popolani grassi.

* * *

On the sixth day of the month of July of the year 1295, the magnates and great men of the city of Florence, seeing themselves mightily oppressed by the new Ordinances of Justice made by the people—and especially by that ordinance which declares that one kinsman is to be held to account for another, and that two witnesses establish public report—having their own friends in the priorate, gave themselves to breaking down the ordinances of the people. And first they made up their great quarrels amongst themselves, especially between the Adimari and Tosinghi, and between the Mozzi and the Bardi. And this done, on an appointed day, they made a great gathering of folk, and petitioned the Priors to have the said articles amended; whereupon all the people in the city of Florence rose in tumult and rushed to arms; the magnates, on armoured horses themselves, and with their retainers from the country and other troops on foot in great numbers; and one set of them drew up in the piazza of S. Giovanni, over whom Forese degli Adimari held the royal ensign; another set assembled at the Piazza a Ponte, whose ensign was held by Vanni Mozzi; and a third set in the Mercato Nuovo, whose standard Geri Spini held; with intent to overrun the city. The popolani were all in arms, in their ranks, with ensigns and banners, in great numbers; and they barricaded the streets of the city at sundry points to hinder the horsemen from overrunning the place, and they gathered at the palace of the Podestà, and at the house of the Priors, who at that time abode at the house of the Cerchi behind San Brocolo. And the people found themselves in great power and well ordered, with force of arms and folk, and they associated with the Priors, whom they did not trust, a number of the greatest and most powerful and discreet of the popolani of Florence, one for each sesto. Wherefore the magnates had no strength nor power against them, and the people might have overthrown them; but consulting for the best, and to avoid civil battle, by the mediation of certain friars between the better sort of either side, each party disarmed; and the city returned to peace and quiet without any change; the Popolo being left in its state and lordship; save that whereas before the proof of public report was established by two witnesses, it was now laid down that there must be three; and even this was conceded by the Priors against the will of the popolani, and shortly afterwards it was revoked and the old order re-established. But for all that this disturbance was the root and beginning of the dismal and ill estate of the city of Florence which thereafter followed, for thenceforth the magnates never ceased to search for means to beat down the people, to their utmost power; and the leaders of the people sought every way of strengthening the people and abasing the magnates by reinforcing the Ordinances of Justice, and they had the great crossbows taken from the magnates and bought up by the commonwealth;

and many families which were not tyrannical nor of any great power they removed from the number of the magnates and added them to the people, to weaken the power of the magnates and increase that of the people; and when the said Priors went out of office they were struck with cudgels behind and had stones flung at them, because they had consented to favour the magnates; and by reason of these disturbances and changes there was a fresh ordering of the people in Florence, whereof the heads were Mancini and Magalotti, Altoviti, Peruzzi, Acciaioli, Cerretani and many others.

*   *   *

In the said year 1298, the commonwealth and people of Florence began to build the Palace of the Priors, by reason of the differences between the people and the magnates, forasmuch as the city was always in jealousy and commotion, at the election of the Priors afresh every two months, by reason of the factions which had already begun; and the Priors which ruled the city and all the republic, did not feel themselves secure in their former habitation, which was the house of the White Cerchi behind the church of San Brocolo. And they built the said palace where had formerly been the houses of the Uberti, rebels against Florence, and Ghibellines; and on the site of those houses they made a piazza, so that they might never be rebuilt. And they bought other houses from citizens, such as the Foraboschi, and there built the said palace and the tower of the Priors, which was raised upon a tower which was more than fifty cubits high, pertaining to the Foraboschi, and called the Torre della Vacca. And to the end the said palace might not stand upon the ground of the said Uberti, they which had the building of it set it up obliquely; but for all that it was a grave loss not to build it four-square, and further removed from the church of San Piero Scheraggio.

*   *   *

In the said time, our city of Florence was in the greatest and happiest state which had ever been since it was rebuilt, or before, alike in greatness and power and in number of people, forasmuch as there were more than 30,000 citizens in the city, and more than 70,000 men capable of arms in the country within her territory; and she was great in nobility of good knights, and in free populace, and in riches, ruling over the greater part of Tuscany; whereupon the sin of ingratitude, with the instigation of the enemy of the human race, brought forth from the said prosperity pride and corruption, which put an end to the feasts and joyaunce of the Florentines. For hitherto they had been living in many delights and dainties, and in tranquillity and with continual banquets; and every year throughout almost all the city on the first day of May, there were bands and companies of men and of women, with sports and dances. But now it came to pass that through envy there arose factions among the citizens; and one of the chief and greatest began in the sesto of offence, to wit of Porte San Piero, between the house of the Cerchi, and the Donati; on the one side through envy, and on the other through rude ungraciousness. The head of the family of the Cerchi was one Vieri dei Cerchi, and he and those of his house were of great affairs, and powerful, and with great kinsfolk, and were very rich merchants, so that their company was among the largest in the world; these were luxurious, inoffensive, uncultured and ungracious, like folk come in a short time to great estate and power. The head of the family of the Donati was Corso Donati, and he and those of his house were gentlemen and warriors, and of no superabundant riches, but were called by a gibe the Malefami. Neighbours they were in Florence and in the country, and while the one set was envious the other stood on their boorish dignity, so that there arose from the clash a fierce scorn between them, which was greatly inflamed by the ill seed of the White and Black parties from Pistoia. . . . And the said Cerchi were the heads of the White party in Florence, and with them held almost all the house of the Adimari, save the branch of the Cavicciuli; all the house of the Abati, which was then very powerful, and part of them were Guelf and part were Ghibelline; a great part of the Tosinghi, specially the branch of Baschiera; part of the house of the Bardi, and part of the Rossi, and likewise some of the Frescobaldi, and part of the Nerli and of the Mannelli, and all the Mozzi, which then were very powerful in riches and in estate; all those of the house of the Scali, and the greater part of the Gherardini, all the Malispini, and a great part of the Bostichi and Giandonati, of the Pigli, and of the Vecchietti and Arrigucci, and almost all the Cavalcanti, which were a great and powerful house, and all the Falconieri which were a powerful house of the people. And with them took part many houses and families of popolani, and lesser craftsmen, and all the Ghibelline magnates and popolani; and by reason of the great following which the Cerchi had, the government of the city was almost all in their power. On the side of the Blacks were all they of the house of the Pazzi, who may be counted with the Donati as the chiefs, and all the Visdomini and all the Manieri and Bagnesi, and all the Tornaquinci, and the Spini and the Bondelmonti, and the Gianfigliazzi, Agli, and Brunelleschi, and Caviciuli, and the other part of the Tosinghi; all the part that was left of all the Guelf houses named above, for those which were not with the Whites held on the contrary with the Blacks. And thus from the said two parties all the city of Florence and its territory was divided and contaminated. For the which cause, the Guelf party, fearing lest the said parties should be turned to account by the Ghibellines, sent to the court to Pope Boniface, that he might use some remedy. For the which thing the said Pope sent for Vieri de' Cerchi, and when he came before him, he prayed him to make peace with Corso Donati and with his party, referring their differences to him; and he promised him to put him and his followers into great and good estate, and to grant him such spiritual favours as he might ask of him. Vieri, albeit he was in other things a sage knight, in this was but little sage, and was too obstinate and capricious, insomuch that he would grant nought of the Pope's request; saying that he was at war with no man; wherefore he returned to Florence, and the Pope was moved with indignation against him and against his party. It came to pass a little while after that certain both of one party and of the other were riding through the city armed and on their guard, and with the party of the young Cerchi was Baldinaccio of the Adimari, and Baschiera of the Tosinghi, and Naldo of the Gherardini, and Giovanni Giacotti Malispini, with their followers, more than thirty on horseback; and with the young Donati were certain of the Pazzi and of the Spini, and others of their company. On the evening of the first of May, in the year 1300, while they were watching a dance of ladies which was going forward on the piazza of Santa Trinità, one party began to scoff at the other, and to urge their horses one against the other, whence arose a great conflict and confusion, and many were wounded, and, as ill-luck would have it, Ricoverino, son of Ricovero of the Cerchi, had his nose cut off his face; and through the said scuffle that evening all the city was moved with apprehension and flew to arms. This was the beginning of the dissensions and divisions in the city of Florence and in the Guelf party, whence many ills and perils followed on afterwards, as in due time we shall make mention. And for this cause we have narrated thus extensively the origin of this beginning of the accursed White and Black parties, for the great and evil

consequences which followed to the Guelf party, and to the Ghibellines, and to all the city of Florence, and also to all Italy; and
like as the death of Dondelmonte the elder was the beginning of
the Guelf and Ghibelline parties, so this was the beginning of the
great ruin of the Guelf party and of our city. And note, that the
year before these things came to pass, the houses of the commonwealth were built, which began at the foot of the old bridge over
the Arno, and extended towards the fortress of Altafronte, and to do
this they raised the piles at the foot of the bridge, and they had
of necessity to move the statue of Mars; and whereas at the first it
looked towards the east, it was turned towards the north, wherefore, because of the augury of old, folk said: "May it please God
that there come not great changes therefrom to our city."

Part Five

GERMANY AND THE LOW COUNTRIES

18. Helmhold: The Slaves Beyond the Elbe

One of the more important developments of the High Middle Ages was the expansion of the Germans into Slavic lands beyond the Elbe and the subsequent Christianization and Germanization of this region. This came about partly through the settlement of colonists in the area and partly through the absorption of the Slavs into the fabric of German civilization. In this selection from *The Chronicle of the Slavs*, written by the priest, Helmhold, who probably died about 1177, we find a contemporary account of this process. It is interesting to note the way in which the Church had to be forcibly maintained in frontier districts and why the Slavs resisted what they felt, quite rightly, was German-Saxon arrogance. One also finds here an excellent description of the German settlement of Lübeck, which later helped make this city one of the great ports in the Baltic. Finally, in the story of the young girl possessed of a demon, we find an excellent example of the superstitious side of popular Christianity during this period. [From *The Chronicle of the Slavs* by Helmhold, trans. Francis J. Tschan (New York: Columbia University Press, 1935), pp. 81–85 and 163–169. Copyright 1935 and © 1968 by Columbia University Press. Reprinted with the omission of footnotes by permission of the publisher.]

About the same time ended the year of the incarnation of the Word, 1001, in which the most valiant emperor Otto III sank, overtaken by an untimely death, after he had thrice entered Rome a victor. There succeeded him on the throne the most pious Henry, remarkable for his justice and sanctity, the one, let me recall, who

founded the bishopric of Bamberg and provided for churchly worship with the amplest munificence. In the tenth year of Henry's
reign the duke of Saxony died, Benno, a man conspicuous for his
thorough probity and zealous defense of the churches. Bernhard,
his son, inherited his princely dignity; he departed, however, from
his father's happy courses. Discord and turbulence never ceased in
this country from the time he was established as duke, for the
reason that in presuming to rise against the emperor Henry he
moved all Saxony to rebel with him against the Caesar.[1] Then he
rose against Christ and brought terror and confusion upon all the
churches of Saxony, those especially that would not join in the
malicious rebellion I have noted. In addition to these misfortunes
this duke, entirely unmindful of the esteem in which both his father
and his grandfather had held the Slavs, through his avarice cruelly
oppressed the nation of the Winuli and sheerly drove it into paganism. At that time Margrave Dietrich and Duke Bernhard held
dominion over the Slavs, the former possessing the eastern country,
the latter, the western. Their villainy forced the Slavs into apostasy.
This heathen folk, still immature in the faith, had previously been
treated with great lenience by the most noble princes who had
tempered their rigor toward those about whose salvation they were
zealously concerned. Now, however, they were pursued by the margrave and Duke Bernhard with such cruelty that they finally threw
off the yoke of servitude and had to take up arms in defense of
their freedom. Mistivoi and Mizzidrag were the chiefs of the Winuli
under whose leadership the rebellion flared up. Now the story goes,
and it is ancient lore, that this Mistivoi sought and was promised
the hand of Duke Bernhard's niece. Then the chief of the Winuli
in his desire to show he was worthy of the engagement with a
thousand horsemen accompanied the duke into Italy and there
nearly all of them were killed. When he returned from the expedition, he asked for the maiden who had been promised to him, but
Margrave Dietrich opposed the plan, vociferating that a kinswoman
of the duke should not be given to a dog. On hearing this the Slav
chieftain departed in great indignation. When, therefore, the duke
had taken other counsel and had sent messengers after him to say
that the desired nuptials might taken place, Mistivoi is said to have
answered: "It is only right that the highborn niece of a great prince
should be married to a man of exalted rank and not, indeed, be
given to a dog. The great thanks that are given us for our service
is that we are now considered dogs, not men. Well then, if the dog

[1] [That is, the emperor Henry II (1002–24)—ED.]

be hale he will take big bites." And with these words he returned
into Slavia. First of all he went to the city of Rethra, which is in
the land of the Lutici, called together all the Slavs who lived to the
eastward and made known to them the insult that had been offered
him and that in the language of the Saxons the Slavs are called
"dogs." But they said: "You, who spurned your co-tribesmen and
courted the Saxons, a perfidious and avaricious race, suffer this
deservedly. Swear, now, to us that you will give them up and we
will stand by you." And he swore to them.

Therefore, after Duke Bernhard had for apparent reasons taken
up arms against the Caesar, the Slavs embraced the opportunity
to collect an army and wasted first the whole of Nordalbingia with
fire and sword. Then, roving about the rest of Slavia, they burned
all the churches and destroyed them even to the ground. They
murdered the priests and the other ministers of the churches with
diverse tortures and left not a vestige of Christianity beyond the
Elbe. At Hamburg, then and later, many clerics and citizens were
led off into captivity and many more were put to death through
hatred of Christianity. The old men of the Slavs who remember all
the deeds of the barbarians tell how Oldenburg had been a city
most populous with Christians. There sixty priests (the rest had
been slaughtered like cattle) were kept as objects of derision. The
oldest of these, the provost of the place, was named Oddar. He and
others were martyred in this manner. After the skin of their heads
had been cut in the form of a cross, the brain of each was laid bare
with an iron. With hands tied behind their backs, the confessors
of God were then dragged through one Slavic town after another
until they died. After having been thus made "a spectacle . . . to
angels and to men," they breathed forth their victorious spirits
in the middle of the course. Many deeds of this kind, which for
lack of written records are now regarded as fables, are remembered
as having been done at this time in the several provinces of the
Slavs and Nordalbingians. In fine, there were so many martyrs in
Slavia that they can hardly be enumerated in a book.

All the Slavs who dwelt between the Elbe and the Oder and
who had practiced the Christian religion for seventy years and more,
that is, during the whole time of the reigns of the Ottos, in this
manner cut themselves off from the body of Christ and of the
Church with which they had before been united. Oh, truly the
judgments of God over men are hidden: "Therefore hath He
mercy on whom He will . . . and whom He will, He hardeneth."
Marveling at His omnipotence, we see those who were the first to

believe falling back into paganism; those, however, who seemed to be the very last, converted to Christ. But He, "the just judge, strong and patient," who of old wiped out in the sight of Israel the seven tribes of Canaan, and kept only the strangers in whom He tried Israel—He, I say, willed now to harden a small part of the heathen through whom He might confound our perfidy. These things were done in the last days of Archbishop Libentius, the elder, under Duke Bernhard, the son of Benno, who grievously oppressed the Slavic people. Dietrich, the margrave of the Slavs, who was as avaricious and as cruel as the one mentioned, was driven from his post and from all his inheritance, and he ended his life as a prebendary at Magdeburg with the bad death he deserved. Mistivoi, the chieftain of the Slavs, was toward the end of his time brought to repentance and converted to God. Since he would not give up Christianity, he was driven from his fatherland and fled to the Bardi with whom he lived as a believer to an old age.

*   *   *

[Some years later in 1137 when] disturbances were breaking out everywhere in Saxony, Pribislav of Lübeck with the band of robbers that he had brought together seized the opportunity utterly to destroy the suburb of Segeberg and all the surrounding hamlets in which the Saxons dwelt. The new oratory and the recently constructed monastery were then consumed by fire, and Volker, a brother of great simplicity, was pierced through by the sword. The other brethren, who escaped, fled for refuge to the haven of Faldera. The priest Ludolph, however, and those who lived with him at Lübeck were not dispersed in this devastation because they lived in the stronghold and under the protection of Pribislav. Nevertheless, they were in a difficult position at a difficult time and in full dread of death. Besides being in want and daily in danger for their lives they were forced to see the chains and the various kinds of torture inflicted on the worshipers of Christ, whom the robber band was wont to capture here and there. Not long afterward a certain Race, of the seed of Cruto, thinking that he would find his enemy Pribislav at Lübeck, came with a fleet of ships. For the two kindred of Cruto and of Henry were in contention over the principate. Since, however, Pribislav still happened to be absent, Race and his men demolished the fortress and its environs. The priests saved themselves by hiding in the reeds until they found refuge at Faldera.

The venerable priest Vicelin and the other preachers of the Word

were, therefore, filled with grievous sadness because the new planta-
tion languished in its very beginnings. But they stayed in the
church at Faldera, constantly intent upon their prayers and fasting.
With what austerity, indeed, with what temperance of food and
every perfection of conduct this group at Faldera was particularly
distinguished can not be adequately stated. The Lord, therefore,
gave them the grace of healing in the measure He had promised—
to cure the sick and to drive out demons. What shall I say about
those who had been seized by a devil? The house was so full of the
obsessed who had been brought from far and wide that the brethren could not rest for their crying out that the presence of the
saintly men kindled their fires. But who came there and was not
freed by the grace of God? In those days it happened that a certain
virgin named Ymme was vexed by a demon and she was brought
to Vicelin, the priest. When the latter plied the demon with questions, why he, the author of corruption, presumed to defile an
incorrupt vessel, he answered in a distinct voice, "Because she has
thrice offended me." "How," asked Vicelin, "has she offended you?"
"Because," the demon replied, "she has hindered my business. For
twice did I send thieves to break into a house, but she, sitting by
the hearth, frightened them away with her cries. Now also, as I was
about to perform a task in Denmark for our prince, I met her on
the way, and in revenge for having been a third time thwarted, I
entered into her." But when the man of God heaped upon him the
words of conjuration, the demon said: "Why do you drive me out
who am ready to depart of my own accord? Now I shall go off to a
nearby village to visit my fellows who are lurking there. This com-
mission, indeed, I received before I set out for Denmark." "What,"
asked Vicelin, "is your name? And who are your confederates and
with whom do they dwell?" "I," replied he, "am called Rufinus.
Furthermore, the comrades about whom you inquire are two: one
is with Rothest, the other with a certain woman of the same town.
I shall visit them today. Tomorrow before the church bell sounds
the first hour I shall return hither to bid adieu, and only then shall
I proceed to Denmark."

When the demon had spoken these words he went out; and the
virgin was freed from the sufferings of her vexation. Then the priest
ordered her to be refreshed and brought back to the church on the
morrow before the hour of prime. When her parents brought her
to the church the next morning, the first hour began to strike
before they stepped on the threshold, and the virgin began to be

troubled. Nevertheless, the diligence of the good pastor did not cease until the spirit departed, overcome by the prevailing might of God. Events, moreover, proved that which the demon had foretold about Rothest, for he strangled himself with a noose soon after he was violently seized with the malignant spirit. In Denmark, also, so serious a disturbance broke out after Eric was slain that it could be plainly seen that a great demon had come there to afflict that people. For who does not know that wars and storms, plagues and other misfortunes of mankind are brought about by the machinations of demons?

As in Denmark so also in Saxony there raged the manifold storms of war; to wit intestine conflicts between the great princes, Henry the Lion [the Proud] and Albert, who were contending for the duchy of Saxony. Above all, however, the Slavic fury, raging as if the leashes were broken because of the preoccupation of the Saxons, disturbed the land of the Holzatians so much that the country of Faldera was reduced almost to a solitude by the murders and the plundering of villages that took place every day. In this time of distress and tribulation the priest Vicelin exhorted the people to place their trust [in God], to recite the litanies in fasting and attrition of heart because evil days were upon them.

Now Henry, who governed the country, a man strenuous at arms and impatient of inactivity, secretly brought together an army of Holzatians and Sturmarians and invaded Slavia in the winter. Attacking those who were next to hand and who were like thorns piercing the eyes of the Saxons, he made a great slaughter of them in all the territory, to wit, of Plön, Lütjenburg, Oldenburg, and the whole of the country which begins at the River Schwale and is encompassed by the Baltic Sea and the River Trave. In one incursion with plunder and fire they wasted all that region except the cities which were fortified with walls and bars and required the more onerous exertion of a siege. The following summer the Holzatians, spurring one another on, went up to the stronghold Plön, even without the count. With the help of Divine Providence and contrary to their expectation they took this fortress, which was stronger than the others, and put the Slavs who were in it to the sword. That year they waged a very successful war and in frequent incursions devastated the country of the Slavs. They did to the Slavs what the Slavs had set themselves to do to them: all their land was reduced to a wilderness.

The Holzatians regarded this Transalbian war of the Saxons as a fortunate event in that it had given them opportunity to avenge themselves on the Slavs without interference from anyone. The princes were accustomed to watch over the Slavs for the purpose of increasing their incomes. After Henry, the son-in-law of King Lothar, had with the assistance of his mother-in-law, the empress Richenza, obtained the duchy and driven Albert, his nephew, out of Saxony, Count Adolph returned into his county. When Henry of Badwide saw that he could not hold out, he set fire to the fortress of Segeberg and to the very strong citadel of Hamburg which the mother of Count Adolph had built of masonry that it might strengthen the city against the attacks of the barbarians. The cathedral there and every noble structure which the elder Adolph had built, Henry also destroyed as he was meditating flight. Henry[2] the Lion then began to arm against Conrad, the king, and led an army against him into Thuringia to a place which is called Kreuzburg. However, as the war was protracted by a truce, the duke returned into Saxony and died not many days thereafter. His son Henry the Lion, who was still a little boy, received the duchy. At this time Lady Gertrude, the boy's mother, gave the province of Wagria to Henry of Badwide for a sum of money. She wished to make trouble for Count Adolph because she disliked him. But as the same lady afterwards married Henry, the brother of King Conrad, and withdrew from the affairs of the duchy, Count Adolph went to the boy duke and his councillors to plead his case for the province of Wagria. He prevailed, both because of the greater justice of his cause and his greater abundance of money. The dissensions which existed between Adolph and Henry were, therefore, thus composed: Adolph got possession of Segeberg and the whole province of the Wagiri; Henry received in compensation Ratzeburg and the land of the Polabi.

Matters having been arranged in this manner, Adolph began to rebuild the fortress at Segeberg and girded it with a wall. As the land was without inhabitants, he sent messengers into all parts, namely, to Flanders and Holland, to Utrecht, Westphalia, and Frisia, proclaiming that whosoever were in straits for lack of fields should come with their families and receive a very good land,—a spacious land, rich in crops, abounding in fish and flesh and exceeding good pasturage. To the Holzatians and Sturmarians he said:

[2] [Henry the Proud, duke of Saxony—ED.]

Have you not subjugated the land of the Slavs and bought it with the blood of your brothers and fathers? Why, then, are you the last to enter into possession of it? Be the first to go over into a delectable land and inhabit it and partake of its delights, for the best of it is due you who have wrested it from the hands of the enemy.

An innumerable multitude of different peoples rose up at this call and they came with their families and their goods into the land of Wagria to Count Adolph that they might possess the country which he had promised them. First of all the Holzatians received abodes in the safest places to the west in the region of Segeberg along the River Trave, also the Bornhöved open and everything extending from the River Schwale as far as Agrimesov and the Plöner-See. The Westphalians settled in the region of Dargune, the Hollanders around Eutin, and the Frisians around Süssel. The country about Plön, however, was still uninhabited. Oldenburg and Lütjenburg and the rest of the lands bordering on the sea he gave to the Slavs to live in, and they became tributary to him.

Count Adolph came later to a place called Bucu and found there the wall of an abandoned fortress which Cruto, the tyrant of God, had built, and a very large island, encircled by two rivers. The Trave flows by on one side, the Wakenitz on the other. Each of these streams has swampy and pathless banks. On the side, however, on which the land road runs there is a little hill surmounted by the wall of the fort. When, therefore, the circumspect man saw the advantages of the site and beheld the noble harbor, he began to build there a city. He called it Lübeck, because it was not far from the old port and city which Prince Henry had at one time constructed. He sent messengers to Niclot, prince of the Abodrites, to make friends with him, and by means of gifts drew to himself all men of consequence, to the end that they would all strive to accommodate themselves to him and to bring peace upon his land. Thus the deserted places of the land of Wagria began to be occupied and the number of its inhabitants was multiplied. Vicelin, the priest, too, on the invitation as well as with the assistance of the count, got back the properties about the fortress of Segeberg which the emperor Lothar had in times past given him for the construction of a monastery and for the support of servants of God. . . .

19. Galbert of Bruges: The Murder of Charles the Good

This account of the murder of Count Charles of Flanders and the disorders which ensued between 1127 and 1128 is interesting for a number of reasons. Its author, Galbert, was a town notary, who may have been a clerk in minor orders, but whose outlook was essentially urban, like Villani of Florence later on. He represented the new power of the burgesses of his native Bruges. Furthermore one can see, in the story of the rise to power of the humble family of Erembalds, the fluidity of classes and groups in early twelfth-century Europe. They are the villains of the story, and their desperate struggle to maintain themselves culminated in their murder of Count Charles. One also senses how fragile the bond of feudal loyalty really was, as compared to that of family solidarity. Thus the realities of place and power are clearly shown in this account in contrast to the theories upon which medieval society was supposed to rest. [From *The Murder of Charles the Good, Count of Flanders* by Galbert of Bruges, revised edition, trans. James Bruce Ross (New York: Columbia University Press, 1968), pp. 102–17. Copyright © 1968 by Columbia University Press. Reprinted with the omission of footnotes by permission of the publisher.]

When strife and conflict broke out between his nephews and those of Thancmar, whose side the count[1] justly favored, the provost was delighted because it gave him an opportunity to betray the count, for he had called to the aid of his nephews all the knights of our region, using money, influence, and persuasion. They besieged Thancmar on all sides in the place where he had entrenched himself, and finally with a considerable force strongly attacked those within. Breaking the bolts of the gates, they cut down the orchards and hedges of their enemies. Though the provost did not take part and acted as if he had done nothing, he actually did everything by direction and deception. He pretended in public that he was full of good will and told his enemies that he grieved to see his nephews engaged in so much strife and killing, although he himself had incited them to all these crimes. In that conflict many on both sides

[1] [Count Charles of Flanders (1118–27)—ED.]

fell on that day wounded or dead. When the provost had learned
that this fight was going on, he himself went to the carpenters who
were working in the cloister of the brothers and ordered that their
tools, that is, their axes, should be taken to that place for use in
cutting down the tower and orchards and houses of his enemies.
Then he sent around to various houses in the town to collect axes
which were quickly taken to that place. And when in the night
his nephews had returned with five hundred knights and squires
and innumerable footsoldiers, he took them into the cloister and
refectory of the brothers where he entertained them all with various
kinds of food and drink and was very happy and boastful about the
outcome.

And while he was harassing his enemies in this way, spending
a great deal in support of those who were helping his nephews,
first the squires and then the knights began to plunder the peasants, even seizing and devouring the flocks and cattle of the country
people. The nephews of the provost were forcibly seizing the be-
longings of the peasants and appropriating them for their own use.
But none of the counts from the beginning of the realm had allowed such pillaging to go on in the realm, because great slaughter
and conflict come to pass in this way.

When the country people heard that the count had come to
Ypres, about two hundred of them went to him secretly and at
night, and kneeling at his feet begged him for his customary paternal
help. They entreated him to order their goods to be returned to
them, that is, their flocks and herds, clothes and silver, and all the
other furniture of their houses which the nephews of the provost
had seized together with those who had fought with them con-
tinuously in that attack and siege. After listening solemnly to the
complaints of those appealing to him, the count summoned his
counselors, and even many who were related to the provost, asking
them by what punishment and with what degree of severity justice
should deal with this crime. They advised him to burn down Borsiard's house without delay because he had plundered the peasants
of the count, and therefore strongly urged him to destroy that
house because as long as it stood, so long would Borsiard indulge
in fighting and pillaging and even killing, and would continue to
lay waste the region. And so the count, acting on this advice, went
and burned the house and destroyed the place to its foundations.
Then that Borsiard and the provost and their accomplices were beside themselves with anxiety both because in this act the count had
clearly lent aid and comfort to their enemies and because the count

was daily disquieting them about their servile status and trying in every way to establish his rights over them.

After burning the house the count went on to Bruges. When he had settled down in his house, his close advisers came to him and warned him, saying that the nephews of the provost would betray him because now they could claim as pretext the burning of the house, although even if the count had not done this they were going to betray him anyway. After the count had eaten, mediators came and appealed to him on behalf of the provost and his nephews, begging the count to turn his wrath from them and to receive them mercifully back into his friendship. But the count replied that he would act justly and mercifully toward them if they would henceforth give up their fighting and pillaging; and he assured them, moreover, that he would certainly compensate Borsiard with a house that was even better. He swore, however, that as long as he was count, Borsiard should never again have any property in that place where the house had been burned up, because as long as he lived there near Thancmar he would never do anything but fight and feud with his enemies, and pillage and slaughter the people.

The mediators, some of whom were aware of the treachery, did not bother the count very much about the reconciliation, and since the servants were going about offering wine they asked the count to have better wine brought in. When they had drunk this, they kept on asking to be served again still more abundantly, as drinkers usually do, so that when they had finally received the very last grant from the count they could go off as if to bed. And by the order of the count everyone present was abundantly served with wine until, after receiving the final grant, they departed.

Then Isaac and Borsiard, William of Wervik, Ingran, and their accomplices, after receiving the assent of the provost, made haste to carry out what they were about to do, by the necessity of divine ordination, through free will. For immediately those who had been mediators and intercessors between the count and the kinsmen of the provost went to the provost's house and made known the count's response, that is, that they had not been able to secure any mercy either for the nephews or their supporters, and that the count would treat them only as the opinion of the leading men of the land had determined in strict justice.

Then the provost and his nephews withdrew into an inner room and summoned those whom they wanted. While the provost guarded the door, they gave their right hands to each other as a pledge that they would betray the count, and they summoned the young Robert to join in the crime, urging him to pledge by his hand that he would share with them what they were about to do and what they had pledged by their hands. But the noble young man, forewarned by the virtue of his soul and perceiving the gravity of what they were urging upon him, resisted them, not wishing to be drawn unwittingly into their compact until he could find out what it was they had bound themselves to do; and while they were pressing him, he turned away and hurried toward the door. But Isaac and William and the others called out to the provost guarding the door not to let Robert leave until by the pressure of his authority Robert should do what they had demanded. The young man, quickly influenced by the flattery and threats of the provost, came back and gave his hand on their terms, not knowing what he was supposed to do with them, and, as soon as he was pledged to the traitors he inquired what he had done. They said:

"We have now sworn to betray that Count Charles who is working for our ruin in every way and is hastening to claim us as his serfs, and you must carry out this treachery with us, both in word and in deed."

Then the young man, struck with terror and dissolved in tears, cried out:

"God forbid that we should betray one who is our lord and the count of the fatherland. Believe me, if you do not give this up, I shall go and openly reveal your treachery to the count and to everyone, and, God willing, I shall never lend aid and counsel to this pact!"

But they forcibly detained him as he tried to flee from them, saying:

"Listen, friend, we were only pretending to you that we were in earnest about that treachery so that we could try out whether you want to stay by us in a certain serious matter; for there is something we have concealed from you up to this point, in which you are bound to us by faith and compact, which we shall tell you about in good time."

And so turning it off as a joke, they concealed their treachery.

Now each one of them left the room and went off to his own place. When Isaac had finally reached home, he pretended to go to bed, for he was awaiting the silence of the night, but soon he remounted his horse and returned to the castle. After stopping at Borsiard's lodgings and summoning him and the others whom he wanted, they went secretly to another lodging, that of the knight, Walter. As soon as they had entered, they put out the fire that burning in the house so that those who had been awakened in the house should not find out from the light of the fire who they were and what sort of business they were carrying on at that time of night, contrary to custom. Then, safe in the darkness, they took counsel about the act of treason to be done as soon as dawn came, choosing for this crime the boldest and rashest members of Borsiard's household, and they promised them rich rewards. To the knights who would kill the count they offered four marks and to the servingmen who would do the same, two marks, and they bound themselves by this most iniquitous compact. Then Isaac returned to his home about daybreak, after he had put heart into them by his counsel and made them ready for such a great crime.

Therefore when day had dawned, so dark and foggy that you could not distinguish anything a spear's length away, Borsiard secretly sent several serfs out into courtyard of the count to watch for his entrance into the church. The count had arisen very early and had made offerings to the poor in his own house, as he was accustomed to do, and so was on his way to church. But as his chaplains reported, the night before, when he had settled down in bed to go to sleep, he was troubled by a kind of anxious wakefulness; perplexed and disturbed in mind, he was so disquieted by the many things on his mind that he seemed quite exhausted, even to himself, now lying on one side, now sitting up again on the bed. And when he had set out on his way toward the church of Saint Donatian, the serfs who had been watching for his exit ran back and told the traitors that the count had gone up into the gallery of the church with a few companions. Then that raging Borsiard and his knights and servants, all with drawn swords beneath their cloaks, followed the count into the same gallery, dividing into two groups so that not one of those whom they wished to kill could escape from the gallery by either way, and behold! they saw the count prostrate before the altar, on a low stool, where he was chanting psalms to God and at the same time devoutly offering prayers and giving out pennies to the poor.

Now it should be known what a noble man and distinguished ruler those impious and inhuman serfs betrayed! His ancestors were among the best and most powerful rulers who from the beginning of the Holy Church had flourished in France, or Flanders, or Denmark, or under the Roman Empire. From their stock the pious count was born in our time and grew up from boyhood to perfect manhood, never departing from the noble habits of his royal ancestors or their natural integrity of life. And before he became count, after performing many notable and distinguished deeds, he took the road of holy pilgrimage to Jerusalem. After crossing the depths of the sea and suffering many perils and wounds for the love of Christ, he at last fulfilled his vow and with great joy reached Jerusalem. Here he also fought strenuously against the enemies of the Christian faith. And so, after reverently adoring the sepulcher of the Lord, he returned home. In the hardship and want of this pilgrimage the pious servant of the Lord learned, as he often related when he was count, in what extreme poverty the poor labor, and with what pride the rich are exalted, and finally with what misery the whole world is affected. And so he made it his habit to stoop to the needy, and to be strong in adversity, not puffed up in prosperity; and as the Psalmist teaches, "The king's strength loves judgment," he ruled the county according to the judgment of the barons and responsible men.

When the life of such a glorious prince had undergone martyrdom, the people of all lands mourned him greatly, shocked by the infamy of his betrayal. Marvelous to tell, although the count was killed in the castle of Bruges on the morning of one day, that is, the fourth day of the week, the news of this impious death shocked the citizens of London, which is in England, on the second day afterwards about the first hour; and towards evening of the same second day it disturbed the people of Laon who live far away from us in France. We learned this through our students who at that time were studying in Laon, as we also learned it from our merchants who were busy carrying on their business on that very day in London. For no one could have spanned these intervals of time or space so quickly either by horse or by ship.

It was ordained by God that bold and arrogant descendants of Bertulf's ancestors should be left behind to carry out the crime of treachery. The others, prevented by death, were influential men in the fatherland in their lifetime, persons of eminence and of great wealth, but the provost passed his life among the clergy, extremely severe and not a little proud. For it was his habit when someone whom he knew perfectly well came into his presence, to dissemble, in his pride, and to ask disdainfully of those sitting near him, who that could be, and then only, if it pleased him, would he greet the newcomer. When he had sold a canonical prebend to someone he would invest him with it not by canonical election but rather by force, for not one of his canons dared to oppose him either openly or secretly. In the house of the brothers in the church of Saint Donatian the canons had formerly been deeply religious

men and perfectly educated, that is, at the beginning of the provost-
ship of this most arrogant prelate. Restraining his pride, they had
held him in check by advice and by Catholic doctrine so that he
could not undertake anything unseemly in the church. But after
they went to sleep in the Lord, the provost, left to himself, set in
motion anything that pleased him and toward which the force of
his pride impelled him. And so when he became head of his family,
he tried to advance beyond everyone in the fatherland his nephews
who were well brought up and finally girded with the sword of
knighthood. Trying to make their reputation known everywhere,
he armed his kinsmen for strife and discord; and he found enemies
for them to fight in order to make it known to everyone that he
and his nephews were so powerful and strong that no one in the
realm could resist them or prevail against them. Finally, accused
in the presence of the count of servile status, and affronted by the
efforts of the count himself to prove that he and all his lineage
were servile, he tried, as we have said, to resist servitude by every
course and device and to preserve his usurped liberty with all his
might. And when, steadfast in his determination, he could not succeed otherwise, he himself, with his kinsmen, carried through the
treachery, which he had long refused to consider, with frightful
consequences involving both his own kinsmen and the peers of
the realm.

But the most pious Lord thought fit to recall His own by the
terror of omens, for in our vicinity bloody water appeared in the
ditches, as a sign of future bloodshed. They could have been called
back from their crime by this if their hardened hearts had not
already entered into a conspiracy for betraying the count. They
often asked themselves, if they killed the count, who would avenge
him? But they did not know what they were saying, for "who," an
infinite word, meant an infinite number of persons, who cannot be
reckoned in a definitive figure; the fact is that the king of France
with a numerous army and also the barons of our land with an
infinite multitude came to avenge the death of the most pious count!
Not even yet has the unhappy consequence of this utterance reached
an end, for as time goes on they do not cease to avenge the death
of the count upon all the suspect and the guilty and those who have
fled in all directions and gone into exile. And so we, the inhabitants
of the land of Flanders, who mourn the death of such a great
count and prince, ever mindful of his life, beg, admonish, and beseech you, after hearing the true and reliable account of his life
and death (that is, whoever shall have heard it), to pray earnestly

for the eternal glory of the life of his soul and his everlasting blessedness with the saints. In this account of his passion, the reader will find the subject divided by days and the events of those days, up to the vengeance, related at the end of this little work. . . .

Part Six

THE NORTH AND
NORTHWEST

20. Snorri Sturluson: Olaf Tryggvason and the Battle of Svolder

Among the more colorful elements of the population of Europe during the middle ages were the Vikings of Scandinavia, the exploits of whose kings are celebrated in *The Heimskringla*, composed by the great Icelandic poet Snorri Sturluson early in the thirteenth century. Snorri, of course, based his accounts on an older oral tradition which we now believe to be closely in accord with the facts as revealed by other sources of information. This selection from his work concerns the most famous naval battle of Scandinavian history, that of Svolder, in which Norway's King Olaf Tryggvason fought bravely until his death against an overwhelmingly larger combined armada of Swedes, Danes, and Norwegians.

What stands out in this account is the bravery of the Norse king, a former Viking, as he fatalistically battles his enemies on his great Drekkar or Dragon Ship, called the Long Serpent. Sensing his spirit one can understand how for centuries Viking raiders were able to terrorize the coasts of Europe as they looted and plundered. [From *The Heimskringla* by Snorri Sturluson, trans. Samuel Laing, 2nd edition trans. R. B. Anderson (London: John C. Nimmo, 1889), pp. 214–24.]

When Earl Sigvalde with his vessels rowed in under the island, Thorkel Dydril of the Crane, and other ship commanders who sailed with him, saw that he turned his ships towards the isle, and thereupon let fall the sails, and rowed after him, calling out, and asking why he sailed that way. The Earl answered, that he was waiting for King Olaf,[1] as he feared there were enemies in the way. They lay upon their oars until Thorkel Nefia came up with the Short Serpent and the three ships which followed him. When they told him the same they too struck sail, and let the ships drive, waiting for King Olaf. But when the king sailed in towards the isle, the whole enemies' fleet came rowing within them out to the Sound. When they saw this they begged the king to hold on his way, and not risk battle with so great a force. The king replied, high on the quarter-deck where he stood, "Strike the sails; never shall men of mine think of flight. I never fled from battle. Let God dispose of my life, but flight I shall never take." It was done as the king commanded. Halfred tells of it thus:

> And far and wide the saying bold
> Of the brave warrior shall be told.
> The king, in many a fray well tried,
> To his brave champions round him cried,
> "My men shall never learn from me
> From the dark weapon-cloud to flee."
> Nor were the brave words spoken then
> Forgotten by his faithful men.

King Olaf ordered the war-horns to sound for all his ships to close up to each other. The king's ship lay in the middle of the line, and on one side lay the Little Serpent, and on the other the Crane; and as they made fast the stems together, the Long Serpent's stem and the Short Serpent's were made fast together; but when the king saw it he called out to his men, and ordered them to lay the larger ship more in advance, so that its stern should not lie so far behind in the fleet.

Then says Ulf the Red, "If the Long Serpent is to lie as much more ahead of the other ships as she is longer than them, we shall have hard work of it here on the forecastle."

The king replies, "I did not think I had a forecastle man afraid as well as red."

Says Ulf, "Defend thou the quarterdeck as I shall the forecastle."

The king had a bow in his hands, and laid an arrow on the string, and aimed at Ulf.

[1] [Olaf Tryggvason (996–1000), King of Norway just before St. Olaf (1016–28) —Ed.]

Ulf said, "Shoot another way, king, where it is more needful: my work is thy gain."

King Olaf stood on the Serpent's quarterdeck, high over the others. He had a gilt shield, and a helmet inlaid with gold; over his armour he had a short red coat, and was easy to be distinguished from other men. When King Olaf saw that the scattered forces of the enemy gathered themselves together under the banners of their ships, he asked, "Who is the chief of the force right opposite to us?"

He was answered, that it was King Svein with the Danish army.

The king replies, "We are not afraid of these soft Danes, for there is no bravery in them; but who are the troops on the right of the Danes?"

He was answered, that it was King Olaf with the Swedish forces.

"Better it were," says King Olaf, "for these Swedes to be sitting at home killing their sacrifices, than to be venturing under our weapons from the Long Serpent. But who owns the large ships on the larboard side of the Danes?"

"That is Earl Eirik Hakonson," say they.

The king replies, "He, methinks, has good reason for meeting us; and we may expect the sharpest conflict with these men, for they are Norsemen like ourselves."

The kings now laid out their oars, and prepared to attack [1000]. King Svein laid his ship against the Long Serpent. Outside of him Olaf the Swede laid himself, and set his ship's stem against the outermost ship of King Olaf's line; and on the other side lay Earl Eirik. Then a hard combat began. Earl Sigvalde held back with the oars on his ships, and did not join the fray. So says Skule Thorsteinson, who at that time was with Earl Eirik:

> I followed Sigvalde in my youth,
> And gallant Eirik; and in truth,
> Tho' now I am grown stiff and old,
> In the spear-song I once was bold.
> Where arrows whistled on the shore
> Of Svold fiord my shield I bore,
> And stood amidst the loudest clash
> When swords on shields made fearful crash.

And Halfred also sings thus:

> In truth I think the gallant king,
> 'Midst such a foemen's gathering,

Would be the better of some score
Of his tight Throndhjem lads, or more;
For many a chief has run away,
And left our brave king in the fray,
Two great kings' power to withstand,
And one great earl's, with his small band.
The king who dares such mighty deed
A hero for his skald would need.

This battle was one of the severest told of, and many were the people slain. The forecastle men of the Long Serpent, the Little Serpent, and the Crane, threw graplings and stem chains into King Svein's ship, and used their weapons well against the people standing below them, for they cleared the decks of all the ships they could lay fast hold of; and King Svein, and all the men who escaped, fled to other vessels, and laid themselves out of bow-shot. It went with this force just as King Olaf Tryggveson had foreseen. Then King Olaf the Swede laid himself in their place; but when he came near the great ships it went with him as with them, for he lost many men and some ships, and was obliged to get away. But Earl Eirik laid his ship side by side with the outermost of King Olaf's ships, thinned it of men, cut the cables, and let it drive. Then he laid alongside of the next, and fought until he had cleared it of men also. Now all the people who were in the smaller ships began to run into the larger, and the earl cut them loose as fast as he cleared them of men. The Danes and Swedes laid themselves now out of shooting distance all around Olaf's ship; but Earl Eirik lay always close alongside of the ships, and used his swords and battle-axes, and as fast as people fell in his vessel others, Danes and Swedes, came in their place. So says Haldor the Unchristian:

Sharp was the clang of shield and sword,
And shrill the song of spears on board,
And whistling arrows thickly flew
Against the Serpent's gallant crew.
And still fresh foemen, it is said,
Earl Eirik to her long side led;
Whole armies of his Danes and Swedes,
Wielding on high their blue sword-blades.

Then the fight became most severe, and many people fell. But at last it came to this, that all King Olaf Trygveson's ships were cleared of men except the Long Serpent, on board of which all

who could still carry their arms were gathered. Then Earl Eirik
lay with his ship by the side of the Serpent, and the fight went on
with battle-axe and sword. So says Haldor:

> Hard pressed on every side by foes,
> The Serpent reels beneath the blows;
> Crash go the shields around the bow!
> Breast-plates and breasts pierced thro' and thro'!
> In the sword-storm the Holm beside,
> The earl's ship lay alongside
> The king's Long Serpent of the sea—
> Fate gave the earl the victory.

Earl Eirik was in the forehold of his ship, where a cover of
shields had been set up. In the fight, both hewing weapons, sword,
and axe, and the thrust of spears had been used; and all that
could be used as weapon for casting was cast. Some used bows, some
threw spears with the hand. So many weapons were cast into the
Serpent, and so thick flew spears and arrows, that the shields could
scarcely receive them; for on all sides the Serpent was surrounded
by war ships. Then King Olaf's men became so mad with rage,
that they ran on board of the enemies' ships, to get at the people
with stroke of sword and kill them; but many did not lay themselves
so near the Serpent, in order to escape the close encounter with
battle-axe or sword; and thus the most of Olaf's men went overboard and sank under their weapons, thinking they were fighting
on plain ground. So says Halfred:

> The daring lads shrink not from death,—
> O'erboard they leap, and sink beneath
> The Serpent's keel: all armed they leap,
> And down they sink five fathoms deep.
> The foe was daunted at their cheers:
> The king, who still the Serpent steers,
> In such a strait—beset with foes—
> Wanted but some more lads like those.

Einar Tambaskelfer, one of the sharpest of bow-shooters, stood
by the mast, and shot with his bow. Einar shot an arrow at Earl
Eirik, which hit the tiller-end just above the earl's head so hard
that it entered the wood up to the arrow-shaft. The earl looked
that way, and asked if they knew who had shot; and at the same
moment another arrow flew between his hand and his side, and

into the stuffing of the chief's stool, so that the barb stood far out on the other side. Then said the earl to a man called Fin,—but some say he was of Fin (Laplander) race, and was a superior archer, —"Shoot that tall man by the mast." Fin shot; and the arrow hit the middle of Einar's bow just at the moment that Einar was drawing it, and the bow was split in two parts.

"What is that," cried King Olaf, "that broke with such a noise?"

"Norway, king, from thy hands," cried Einar.

"No! not quite so much as that," says the king; "take my bow, and shoot," flinging the bow to him.

Einar took the bow, and drew it over the head of the arrow. "Too weak, too weak," said he, "for the bow of a mighty king!" and, throwing the bow aside, he took sword and shield, and fought valiantly.

The king stood on the gangways of the Long Serpent, and shot the greater part of the day; sometimes with the bow, sometimes with the spear, and always throwing two spears at once. He looked down over the ship's side, and saw that his men struck briskly with their swords, and yet wounded but seldom. Then he called aloud, "Why do ye strike so gently that ye seldom cut?" One among the people answered, "The swords are blunt and full of notches." Then the king went down into the forehold, opened the chest under the throne, and took out many sharp swords, which he handed to his men; but as he stretched down his right hand with them, some observed that blood was running down under his steel glove, but no one knew where he was wounded.

Desperate was the defence in the Serpent, and there was the heaviest destruction of men done by the forecastle crew, and those of the forehold, for in both places the men were chosen men, and the ship was highest; but in the middle of the ship the people were thinned. Now when Earl Eirik saw there were but few people remaining beside the ship's mast, he determined to board; and he entered the Serpent with four others. Then came Hyrning, the king's brother-in-law, and some others against him, and there was the most severe combat; and at last the earl was forced to leap back on board his own ship again, and some who had accompanied him were killed, and others wounded. Thord Kolbeinson alludes to this:

> On Odin's deck, all wet with blood,
> The helm-adorned hero stood;
> And gallant Hyrning honour gained,

Clearing all round with sword deep stained.
The high mountain peaks shall fall,
Ere men forget this to recall.

Now the fight became hot indeed, and many men fell on board the Serpent; and the men on board of her began to be thinned off, and the defence to be weaker. The earl resolved to board the Serpent again, and again he met with a warm reception. When the forecastle men of the Serpent saw what he was doing, they went aft and made a desperate fight; but so many men of the Serpent had fallen, that the ship's sides were in many places quite bare of defenders; and the earl's men poured in all around into the vessel, and all the men who were still able to defend the ship crowded aft to the king, and arrayed themselves for his defence. So says Haldor the Unchristian:

> Eirik cheers on his men,—
> "On to the charge again!"
> The gallant few
> Of Olaf's crew
> Must refuge take
> On the quarter-deck.
> Around the king
> They stand in ring;
> Their shields enclose
> The king from foes,
> And the few who still remain
> Fight madly, but in vain.
> Eirik cheers on his men—
> "On to the charge again!"

Kolbiorn the marshal, who had on clothes and arms like the king's, and was a remarkably stout and handsome man, went up to the king on the quarter-deck. The battle was still going on fiercely even in the forehold. But as many of the earl's men had now got into the Serpent as he could find room, and his ships lay all round her, and few were the people left in the Serpent for defence against so great a force; and in a short time most of the Serpent's men fell, brave and stout though they were. King Olaf and Kolbiorn the marshal both sprang overboard, each on his own side of the ship; but the earl's men had laid out boats around the Serpent, and killed those who leaped overboard. Now when the King had sprung overboard, they tried to seize him with their hands, and bring him to Earl Eirik; but King Olaf threw his shield over his head, and

THE NORTH AND NORTHWEST

sank beneath the waters. Kolbiorn held his shield behind him to protect himself from the spears cast at him from the ships which lay round the Serpent, and he fell so upon his shield that it came under him, so that he could not sink so quickly. He was thus taken and brought into a boat, and they supposed he was the king. He was brought before the earl; and when the earl saw it was Kolbiorn, and not the king, he gave him his life. At the same moment all of King Olaf's men who were in life sprang overboard from the Serpent; and Thorkel Nefia, the king's brother, was the last of all the men who sprang overboard. It is thus told concerning the king by Halfred:

> The Serpent and the Crane
> Lay wrecks upon the main.
> On his sword he cast a glance,—
> With it he saw no chance.
> To his marshal, who of yore
> Many a war-chance had come o'er,
> He spoke a word—then drew in breath,
> And sprang to his deep-sea death.

21. The Greenlanders' Saga: The Vinland Voyages

Quite different from the picture of war and high politics celebrated in the *Saga of Olaf Tryggvason* is that shown here. These episodes from *The Greenlanders' Saga*, which may have been composed in the late twelfth century in Iceland, tell us of humbler folk, Icelanders originally, who settled in Greenland and later on discovered the North American continent and attempted to set up permanent homes there too. They seem to have abandoned this attempt under the threat of Indian and Eskimo attack. The story of all this, in part related here, seems realistic in tone. Indeed, present-day archeological research in Newfoundland and elsewhere and the recent discovery of the Vinland map have tended to substantiate this account from the Sagas. It also helps to prove that Western European medieval man had become an accomplished navigator of the Atlantic long before Columbus sailed westward and had laid the basis of his later control of the seven seas of the world. Finally, this account focuses our attention, not on kings, but on hardy, seafaring farming folk who were able to share with

The next thing that happened [1] was that Bjarni Herjolfsson came over from Greenland to see earl Eirik, and the earl
made him welcome. Bjarni gave an account of those travels of his
on which he had seen these lands, and people thought how lacking
in enterprise and curiosity he had been in that he had nothing to
report of them, and he won some reproach for this. Bjarni became
a retainer of the earl's, and next summer returned to Greenland.

There was now much talk about voyages of discovery. Leif, son
of Eirik the Red of Brattahlid, went to see Bjarni Herjolfsson,
bought his ship from him, and found her a crew, so that they were
thirty-five all told. Leif invited Eirik his father to lead this expedition too, but Eirik begged off rather, reckoning he was now getting
on in years, and was less able to stand the rigours of bad times at
sea than he used to be. Leif argued that of all their family he would
still command the best luck, so Eirik gave way to him, and once
they were ready for their voyage came riding from home. . . .

They now prepared their ship and sailed out to sea once they
were ready, and they lighted on that land first which Bjarni and
his people had lighted on last. They sailed to land there, cast anchor
and put off a boat, then went ashore, and could see no grass there.
The background was all great glaciers, and right up to the glaciers
from the sea as it were a single slab of rock. The land impressed
them as barren and useless. "At least," said Leif, "it has not happened to us as to Bjarni over this land, that we failed to get ourselves ashore. I shall now give the land a name, and call it Hellu-
land, Flatstone Land." After which they returned to the ship.

After that they sailed out to sea and lighted on another land.
This time too they sailed to land, cast anchor, then put off a boat
and went ashore. The country was flat and covered with forest, with
extensive white sands wherever they went, and shelving gently to
the sea. "This land," said Leif, "shall be given a name in accordance
with its nature, and be called Markland, Wood Land." After which
they got back down to the ship as fast as they could.

[1] The narrator means after the death of Olaf Tryggvason at the sea fight at
Svold, in the year 1000. Earl Eirik . . . one of his adversaries there, then became earl of Norway . . . .

From there they now sailed out to sea with a north-east wind and were at sea two days before catching sight of land. They sailed to land, reaching an island which lay north of it, where they went ashore and looked about them in fine weather, and found that there was dew on the grass, whereupon it happened to them that they set their hands to the dew, then carried it to their mouths, and thought they had never known anything so sweet as that was. After which they returned to their ship and sailed into the sound which lay between the island and the cape projecting north from the land itself. They made headway west round the cape. There were big shallows there at low water; their ship went aground, and it was a long way to look to get sight of the sea from the ship. But they were so curious to get ashore they had no mind to wait for the tide to rise under their ship, but went hurrying off to land where a river flowed out of a lake. Then, as soon as the tide rose under their ship, they took their boat, rowed back to her, and brought her up into the river, and so to the lake, where they cast anchor, carried their skin sleeping-bags off board, and built themselves booths. Later they decided to winter there and built a big house.

There was no lack of salmon there in river or lake, and salmon bigger than they had ever seen before. The nature of the land was so choice, it seemed to them that none of the cattle would require fodder for the winter. No frost came during the winter, and the grass was hardly withered. Day and night were of a more equal length there than in Greenland or Iceland. On the shortest day of winter the sun was visible in the middle of the afternoon as well as at breakfast time.

Once they had finished their house-building Leif made an announcement to his comrades. "I intend to have our company divided now in two, and get the land explored. Half our band shall remain here at the hall, and the other half reconnoitre the countryside—yet go no further than they can get back home in the evening, and not get separated." So for a while that is what they did, Leif going off with them or remaining in camp by turns. Leif was big and strong, of striking appearance, shrewd, and in every respect a temperate, fair-dealing man.

One evening it turned out that a man of their company was missing. This was Tyrkir the German. Leif was greatly put out by this, for Tyrkir had lived a long while with him and his father, and had shown great affection for Leif as a child. He gave his shipmates the rough edge of his tongue, then turned out to go and look for him, taking a dozen men with him. But when they had got only a short way from the hall there was Tyrkir coming to meet them. His welcome was a joyous one. Leif could see at once that his foster-father was in fine fettle. He was a man with a bulging forehead. rolling eyes, and an insignificant little face, short and not much to look at, but handy at all sorts of crafts.

"Why are you so late, foster-father," Leif asked him, "and parted this way from your companions?"

By way of a start Tyrkir held forth a long while in German, rolling his eyes all ways, and pulling faces. They had no notion what he was talking about. Then after a while he spoke in Norse. "I went no great way further than you, yet I have a real novelty to report. I have found vines and grapes."

"Is that the truth, foster-father?" Leif asked.

"Of course it's the truth," he replied. "I was born where wine and grapes are no rarity."

They slept overnight, then in the morning Leif made this announcement to his crew. "We now have two jobs to get on with, and on alternate days must gather grapes or cut vines and fell timber, so as to provide a cargo of such things for my ship." They acted upon these orders, and report has it that their towboat was filled with grapes [?raisins]. A full ship's cargo was cut, and in the spring they made ready and sailed away. Leif gave the land a name in accordance with the good things they found in it, calling it Vinland, Wineland; after which they sailed out to sea and had a good wind till they sighted Greenland and the mountains under the glaciers.

*   *   *

There was now much discussion of Leif's expedition to Vinland. His brother Thorvald considered that the land had been explored in too restricted a fashion. So Leif said to Thorvald. "If you want to, go you to Vinland, brother, in my ship; but first I want her to go for the timber which Thorir had on the reef."

That was done, and now Thorvald made preparations for this voyage along with thirty men, under the guidance of Leif his brother. Later they put their ship ready and sailed out to sea, and nothing is recorded of their voyage till they came to Vinland, to Leifsbudir, where they saw to their ship and stayed quiet over the winter, catching fish for their food. But in the spring Thorvald ordered them to make their ship ready, and for the ship's boat and certain of the men to proceed along the west coast and explore there during the summer. It looked to them a beautiful and well-wooded land, the woods scarcely any distance from the sea, with white sands, and a great many islands and shallows. Nowhere did they come across habitation of man or beast, but on an island in the west found a wooden grain-holder. They found no other work of man, so returned and reached Leifsbudir that autumn.

Next summer Thorvald set off eastwards with the merchant-ship and further north along the land. Off a certain cape they met with heavy weather, were driven ashore, and broke the keel from under the ship. They made a long stay there, mending their ship. Said Thorvald to his shipmates: "I should like us to erect the keel on the cape here, and call it Kjalarnes, Keelness." This they did, and afterwards sailed away and east along the land, and into the mouth of the next fjord they came to, and to a headland jutting out there which was entirely covered with forest. They brought the ship to where they could moor her, thrust out a gangway to the shore, and Thorvald walked ashore with his full ship's company. "This is a lovely place," he said, "and here I should like to make my home." Then they made for the ship, and saw three mounds on the sands up inside the headland. They walked up to them and could see three skin-boats there, and three men under each. So they divided forces and laid hands on them all, except for one who got away with his canoe. The other eight they killed, and afterwards walked back to the headland, where they had a good look round and could see various mounds on up the fjord which they judged to be human habitations. Then after this so great a drowsiness overtook them that they could not keep awake, and all fell asleep. Then a cry carried to them, so that they were all roused up, and the words of the cry were these: "Rouse ye, Thorvald, and all your company, if you would stay alive. Back to your ship with all your men, and leave this land as fast as you can!" With that there came from inside the fjord a countless fleet of skin-boats and attacked them. "We must rig up our war-roof," ordered Thorvald, "each side of the ship, and defend ourselves to the utmost, yet offer little by way of attack." Which they did. The Skrælings kept shooting at them for a while, but then fled away, each one as fast as he could.

＊   ＊   ＊

There was now fresh talk of a Vinland voyage, for this appeared an enterprise at once profitable and honourable. The same sum-

mer that Karlsefni returned from Vinland a ship arrived in Greenland from Norway, commanded by two brothers, Helgi and Finnbogi, who stayed there in Greenland over the winter. These
brothers were Icelanders by descent and from the Eastfirths. The
next thing to report is that Freydis Eiriksdottir made a journey
from her home at Gardar; she called to see the brothers Helgi and
Finnbogi, and invited them to take their vessel on an expedition
to Vinland, and have equal shares with her in all such profit as
they might obtain there. They said they would, so from them she
went on to see her brother Leif and asked him to give her the
house he had had built in Vinland. He made his usual answer: he
would lend the house, he said, but not give it. The arrangement
between Freydis and the brothers was this, that they should each
take thirty able-bodied men on their ship, in addition to any
womenfolk; but Freydis immediately showed her disregard for this,
taking an extra five men and so concealing them that the brothers
had no suspicion of it till they reached Vinland.

Now they put to sea, having arranged beforehand that so far as
possible they would sail in company. There was, indeed, little between them, but even so the brothers arrived a shade ahead and
carried their gear up to Leif's house. But once Freydis arrived, they
too unloaded ship and carried their gear up to the house.

"Why have you carried your stuff in here?" Freydis demanded.

"Because we assumed," they said, "the whole arrangement between us would be kept to."

"Leif lent the house to me," she retorted, "not to you."

"We are no match for you in wickedness, we brothers," said
Helgi. They moved their gear out and built their own hall, sitting
it further away from the sea by the lakeside, and making the necessary preparations, while Freydis had timber felled for her ship.

Now winter set in, and the brothers suggested starting games and
holding entertainments to pass the time. That was the way of it
for a while, till there was a turn for the worse between them, and
deep division made, and the games ended, and no coming and
going between the houses. This went on for much of the winter.
Then early one morning Freydis got out of bed and put on her
clothes (but not her shoes and stockings), and such was the weather
that a heavy dew had fallen. She took her husband's cloak, wrapped
it about her, then walked over to the brothers' house, to the door.
A man had gone outside a little earlier and left the door ajar: she
pushed it open, and stood in the entrance a while without saying a
word.

Finnbogi was lying at the innermost end of the hall. He was awake. "What do you want here, Freydis?"

"For you to get up and come outside with me. I want to talk to you."

So that is what he did. They walked to a tree-trunk which lay under the wall of the house, and sat down on it.

"How are you liking things?" she asked him.

"I think the country a good and fruitful one," he replied, "but this cold wind blowing between us, I think that bad, for I swear there is no reason for it."

"As you say," said she. "I think the same. But my business in coming to see you is that I should like to trade ships with you brothers, for you have a bigger one than mine, and I want to get away from here."

"I can meet you on that," he said, "if it will please you."

With that they parted, she went home, and Finnbogi back to bed. She climbed into bed with her cold feet, and at this Thorvard woke, and asked why she was so cold and wet. She answered in a passion. "I have been to those brothers," she said, "asking to buy their ship—I wanted to buy a bigger one. But they took it so badly that they beat me, maltreated me—and you, wretch that you are, will avenge neither my shame nor your own! I can see now that I am not back home in Greenland, but I shall separate from you unless you take vengeance for this."

He could not endure this baiting of hers. He ordered his men to turn out immediately and take their weapons, which they did, and crossed straightway to the brothers' house and marched in on the sleeping men, seized them and bound them, then led them outside, each man as he was bound. And Freydis had each man killed as he came out.

Now all the men were killed, but the women were left, and no one would kill them.

"Hand me an axe," said Freydis.

Which was done, and she turned upon the five women they had there, and left them dead.

After this wicked deed they returned to their own quarters, and it was only too clear that Freydis felt she had handled the situation very well. She had this to say to her companions. "If it is our fate to return to Greenland, I shall be the death of any man who so much as mentions what has taken place. What we must say is that they stayed behind here when we sailed away."

So early in the spring they made ready the ship the brothers had owned, with every valuable commodity they could lay their hands on and the ship carry. Then they sailed to sea, had a good passage, and brought their ship to Eiriksfjord early in the summer. Karlsefni was still there and had his ship ready and waiting to put to sea. He was waiting for a wind, and men maintain that a more richly freighted ship never left Greenland than this one he was captain of.

Freydis now went to her house, for it had taken no harm all this while. She made lavish gifts to all the members of her crew, because she wanted to keep her misdeeds hidden. She now settled down at home. But they were not all so secretive by nature as to keep their mouths shut about their crimes and misdeeds, so that they did not come to light in the end; and eventually it came to the ears of Leif her brother, who thought it a sorry story indeed. He seized three of Freydis's crew and tortured them till they confessed to the whole thing together, and their stories tallied. "I have not the heart," said Leif, "to treat my sister Freydis as she deserves, but I predict this of her and her husband: no offspring of theirs will come to much good." And such proved the case, that from there on no one thought anything but ill of them. . . .

22. Gerald of Wales: The Norman Conquest of Ireland

If the German Drang Nach Osten (Drive to the East) and the discovery of North America were two great events which took place during this period in Northern Europe, a third was the Anglo-Norman conquest of much of Ireland. A churchman of Welsh noble extraction, Bishop Gerald (1146–1223) has left us a remarkable account of this event, of which the following excerpts tell us something of its earlier phases.

In perusing these passages, one should note that the conquest of Ireland began in Wales and was the result of activity by Norman marcher lords of this region who were all but independent of the English crown. Only after it was clear that they had become successful did Henry II follow them to Ireland and take advantage of their victories there. The conquest of Ireland in the twelfth century, then, was an aspect of an advancing Anglo-Norman frontier in the British Isles. Furthermore, it seems ironical to note that the Fitzgerald family, here represented by Maurice Fitzgerald,

who are the ancestors of John and Robert Kennedy, first appeared
in Ireland as Anglo-Norman invaders and conquerors of the native
Irish population. [From *The Historical Works of Giraldus Cam-
briensis,* ed. Thomas Wright, trans. F. Forester (London: Henry G.
Bohn, 1863; George Bell and Sons, 1891), pp. 184–87, 189–92, and
202–4.]

Dermitius [Dermot], the son of Murchard, and prince of
Leinster, who ruled over that fifth part of Ireland, possessed in our
times the maritime districts in the east of the island, separated only
from Great Britain by the sea which flowed between. His youth and
inexperience in government led him to become the oppressor of
the nobility, and to impose a cruel and intolerable tyranny on the
chiefs of the land. This brought him into trouble, and it was not
the only one; for O'Roric, prince of Meath, having gone on an
expedition into a distant quarter, left his wife, the daughter of
Omachlacherlin, in a certain island of Meath during his absence;
and she, who had long entertained a passion for Dermitius [Dermot]
took advantage of the absence of her husband, and allowed herself
to be ravished, not against her will. As the nature of women is
fickle and given to change, she thus became the prey of the spoiler
by her own contrivance. For as Mark Anthony and Troy are witnesses, almost all the greatest evils in the world have arisen from
women. King O'Roric being moved by this to great wrath, but more
for the shame than the loss he suffered, was fully bent on revenge,
and forthwith gathered the whole force of his own people and the
neighbouring tribes, calling besides to his aid Roderic, prince of
Connaught, then monarch of all Ireland. The people of Leinster,
considering in what a strait their prince was, and seeing him beset
on every side by bands of enemies, began to call to mind their own
long-smothered grievances, and their chiefs leagued themselves with
the foes of Mac Murchard, and deserted him in his desperate
fortunes.

Dermitius [Dermot], seeing himself thus forsaken and left destitute, fortune frowning upon him, and his affairs being now desperate, after many fierce conflicts with the enemy, in which he was
always worsted, at length resolved, as his last refuge, to take ship
and flee beyond sea. It is therefore apparent from many occurrences,
that it is safer to govern willing subjects than those who are dis-
obedient. Nero learnt this, and Domitian also, while in our times,
Henry, duke of Saxony and Bavaria, was made sensible of it. . . .

Meanwhile, Mac Murchard, submitting to his change of fortune,
and confidently hoping for some favourable turn, crossed the sea

with a favourable wind, and came to Henry II, king of England, for the purpose of earnestly imploring his succour. Although the king was at that time beyond sea, far away in Aquitaine, in France, and much engaged in business, he received Murchard with great kindness, and the liberality and courtesy which was natural to him; and having heard the causes of his exile and coming over, and received his bond of allegiance and oath of fealty, granted him letters patent to the effect following: "Henry, king of England, duke of Normandy and Aquitaine, and count of Anjou, to all his liegemen, English, Normans, Welsh, and Scots, and to all other nations subject to his dominion, Sendeth, greeting, Whensoever these our letters shall come unto you, know ye that we have received Dermitius [Dermot], prince of Leinster, unto our grace and favour, —Wherefore, whosoever within the bounds of our territories shall be willing to give him aid, as our vassal and liegeman, in recovering his territories, let him be assured of our favour and licence on that behalf."

Dermitius [Dermot], returning through Great Britain, loaded with honourable gifts by the royal munificence, but encouraged more by hope for the future than any aid he had yet obtained, reached at last the noble town of Bristol. Here he sojourned for some time, making a liberal expenditure, as on account of the ships which made frequent voyages from Ireland to that port, he had opportunities of hearing the state of affairs in his own country and among his people. During his stay he caused the royal letters patent to be read several times in public, and made liberal offers of pay and lands to many persons, but in vain. At length, however, Richard, surnamed Strongbow, earl of Strigul, the son of earl Gilbert, came and had a conference with him; and after a prolonged treaty it was agreed between them that in the ensuing spring the earl should lend him aid in recovering his territories, Dermitius [Dermot] solemnly promising to give him his eldest daughter for wife, with the succession to his kingdom.

*   *   *

In the meantime, Robert Fitz-Stephen, [another Norman leader] . . . had mustered thirty men-at-arms, of his own kindred and retainers, together with sixty men in half-armour, and about three hundred archers and foot-soldiers, the flower of the youth of Wales, and embarking them in three ships, landed at the Banne, about the calends of May [A.D. 1170]. Then was the old prophecy of Merlin the Wild fulfilled: "A knight, bipartite, shall first break the bonds of Ireland." If you wish to understand this mysterious prediction, you must have respect to the descent of Robert Fitz-Stephen by both his parents. On the father's side he was an Anglo-Norman, on the mother's a Cambro-Briton, being the son of the noble lady Nesta.

In his company there also came over a man of fallen fortunes, Harvey de Montmaurice, who, having neither armour nor money, was a spy rather than a soldier, and as such acting for earl Richard, whose uncle he was. On the following day, Maurice de Prendergast,[1] a stout and brave soldier, from the district of Ros, in South Wales, following Fitz-Stephen, and having embarked at the port of Milford, with ten men-at-arms, and a large body of archers, in two ships, landed also at the Banne. All these forces having disembarked on the island of the Banne, and finding themselves in a position far from secure, the news of their landing having been spread abroad, they sent messengers to Dermitius [Dermot], apprizing him of their arrival. Meanwhile, some of the people who dwelt on the coast, although they had deserted Dermitius [Dermot], when fortune frowned upon him, when she changed her aspect flocked together to support him. . . .

Mac Murchard, as soon as he heard of their coming, sent forward his natural son, Duvenald, who, though not legitimate, was a man of consequence in his country, to join the English expedition, and followed himself, without loss of time, and in great joy, at the head of five hundred men. Having renewed their former engagements and confirmed them by many oaths mutually exchanged for security on both sides, they joined their forces, and the combined troops of the different races being united in one common object, marched to the attack of the town of Wexford, distant about twelve miles from the Banne. The people of the town, when they heard of this, were so confident in their wonted good fortune, having been hitherto independent, that they sallied forth, to the number of about two thousand men, and meeting the enemy near their camp, resolved on giving them battle. But when they perceived the troops to which they were opposed, arrayed in a manner they had never before witnessed, and a body of horsemen, with their bright armour, helmets, and shields, they adopted new plans with a new state of

[1] [Maurice Fitzgerald, mentioned later on, probably the ancestor of the Kennedys—Ed.]

affairs, and having set fire to, and burnt the suburbs, forthwith retired within their walls.

Fitz-Stephen lost no time in preparing for the attack; and lining the trenches with those of his troops who wore armour, while the archers were posted so as to command the advanced towers, an assault was made on the walls with loud cries and desperate vigour. But the townsmen were ready to stand on their defence, and casting down from the battlements large stones and beams, repulsed the attack for a while, and caused numerous losses. Among the wounded was Robert de Barri, a young soldier, who, inflamed with ardent valour, and dauntless in the face of death, was among the first who scaled the walls; but being struck upon his helmet by a great stone, and falling headlong into the ditch below, narrowly escaped with his life, his comrades with some difficulty drawing him out. . . . Upon this repulse, withdrawing from the walls, they gathered in haste on the neighbouring strand, and forthwith set fire to all the ships they found lying there. Among these, a merchant-ship, lately arrived from the coast of Britain with a cargo of corn and wine, was moored in the harbor; and a band of the boldest youths rowing out in boats, got on board the vessel, but were carried out to sea, the sailors having cut the hawsers from the anchors, and the wind blowing from the west; so that it was not without great risk, and hard rowing after taking to their boats again, that they regained the land.

Thus fortune, constant only in her instability, almost deserted not only Mac Murchard, but Fitz-Stephen also. However, on the following morning, after mass had been celebrated throughout the army, they proceeded to renew the assault with more circumspection and order, relying on their skill as well as their courage; and when they drew near to the walls, the townsmen, despairing of being able to defend them, and reflecting that they were disloyally resisting their prince, sent envoys to Dermitius [Dermot] commissioned to treat of the terms of peace. At length, by the meditation of two bishops, who chanced to be in the town at that time, and other worthy and peaceable men, peace was restored, the townsmen submitting to Dermitius [Dermot], and delivering four of their chief men as hostages for their fealty to him. And the more to animate the courage of his adherents, and reward their chiefs for their first success, he forthwith granted the town, with the whole territory appertaining to it, to Fitz-Stephen and Maurice, according to the stipulations in their original treaty. He also conferred on Hervey de Montmaurice two cantreds lying between the towns of Wexford and Waterford, to hold to him and his heirs in fee.

*   *   *

These matters being settled, and fortune appearing again to smile upon them with a more favourable aspect, behold, Maurice Fitzgerald, of whom I have already spoken . . . and who was half-brother by the mother's side to Robert Fitz-Stephen, landed at Wexford with ten men-at-arms, thirty mounted retainers, and about one hundred archers and foot-soldiers, who came over in two ships. This Maurice was a man much distinguished for his honour and courage, of an almost maidenish modesty, true to his word, and firm in his resolution. Mac Murchard was much delighted and encouraged by the tidings of this new arrival, and calling to mind, with the desire of vengeance, the deep injuries which the people of Dublin had done both to his father and himself, he assembled an army and prepared to march towards Dublin.

In the meantime, Fitz-Stephen was building a fort upon a steep rock, commonly called the Karrec, situated about two miles from Wexford, a place strong by nature, but which art made still stronger. Maurice Fitzgerald, however, with the English troops, joined the army under Dermitius [Dermot], who took the command and acted as guide. In a short time, the whole territory belonging to Dublin, with the adjacent districts, were almost laid waste, and reduced to the last extremity, by the ravages of the enemy, and by fire and sword; so that at length the townsmen sued for peace, and gave security for keeping their allegiance to their prince in time to come, and paying him due homage and service.

Meanwhile, quarrels having broken out between Roderic of Connaught and Duvenald of Limerick, as soon as Roderic with his troops made an irruption on the borders of Limerick, Dermitius [Dermot] despatched Fitz-Stephen and his followers to the relief of Duvenald, who was his son-in-law. Duvenald thus supported, after several battles, in all of which he was victorious, compelled Roderic to retreat with disgrace into his own territories, and freed himself altogether from any acknowledgment of his supremacy. In this expedition, as in all others, Meyler and Robert de Barri distinguished themselves by their extraordinary valour.

*   *   *

Dermitius [Dermot] having received intelligence that the citizens of Dublin had summoned the people from all parts of Ireland to succour them in defending the place, and that all the roads through the woods and other difficult passes were beset with armed men, was careful to avoid his father's mischance, and leading his army by the ridges of the mountains of Glyndelachan (Glendalough), he conducted it in safety to the walls of the city. Dermitius [Dermot] had a mortal hatred for the citizens of Dublin, and not without reason; for they had murdered his father, while sitting in the hall of the house of one of the chief men, which he used for his court of justice; and they added insult to the foul deed by burying his corpse with a dog.

Now, however, on their sending envoys to Dermitius [Dermot], and through the powerful mediation of Laurence, of blessed memory, who was at that time archbishop of Dublin, a truce was agreed upon, during which the terms of a treaty of peace might be settled. Notwithstanding this, Raymond on one side of the city, and on the other a brave soldier, whose name was Milo de Cogan . . . rushed to the walls with bands of youths, eager for the fight, and greedy of plunder, and making a resolute assault, got possession of the place after a great slaughter of the citizens. The better part of them, however, under their king Hasculf, embarked in ships and boats with their most valuable effects, and sailed to the northern islands. . . .

The earl then, having spent a few days in settling order in the city, left Milo de Cogan there as constable, and at the instigation of Mac Murchard, who had not forgotten an ancient feud with O'Roric, king of Meath, made a hostile irruption into the territories of that prince, and the whole of Meath was plundered and laid waste with fire and sword.

Roderic, king of Connaught, perceiving that he was in jeopardy, "when his neighbour's house was on fire," sent envoys to Dermitius [Dermot], with this message: "Contrary to the conditions of our treaty of peace, you have invited a host of foreigners into this island, and yet, as long as you kept within the bounds of Leinster, we bore it patiently. But now, forasmuch as, regardless of your solemn oaths, and having no concern for the fate of the hostage you gave, you have broken the bounds agreed on, and insolently crossed the frontiers of your own territory; either restrain in future the irruptions of your foreign bands, or I will certainly have your son's head cut off, and send it to you." Dermitius [Dermot], having received this message, made an arrogant reply, adding also that he would not desist from the enterprise he had undertaken, until he had reduced Connaught to subjection, which he claimed as his ancient inheritance, and obtained with it the monarchy of the whole of Ireland. Roderic was so indignant at this reply, that he caused the son of Dermitius [Dermot], who had been delivered to him for an hostage . . . to be put to death.

Part Seven

CRUSADE AND TRAVEL

23. Odo of Deuil: Louis VII's Travels Through Germany and Hungary

Odo of Deuil, chaplain to King Louis VII, and later successor to Suger as abbot of Saint Denis, who died in 1162, has managed to give us a rather remarkable account of his royal master's travels through Central Europe on his way to Constantinople during the Second Crusade. We tend to forget that medieval kings were essentially mobile during their reigns—always on the move from one residence or location to another—as a study of the daily itineraries of Henry II of England shows. Thus we need to see them in transit to get an understanding of how they moved and met the challenges of new situations and of a strange and sometimes hostile local population. Louis VII's army in contact with German townsmen and Hungarian political factions gives us a picture of this kind of life. This account also pictures for us political intrigue on the royal level which disturbed every medieval realm just as it did Hungary at the time of Louis VII's travel through its territory. [From *De Profectione Ludovici VII in Orientem* by Odo of Deuil, trans. Virginia G. Berry (New York: Columbia University Press, 1948), pp. 21–39. Copyright 1948 by Columbia University Press. Reprinted with the omission of footnotes by permission of the publisher.]

After the illustrious king's departure from the Church of St. Denis nothing memorable was done in his realm, unless, perhaps, you wish to have recorded the fact that he made the archbishop of Rheims [an] associate in the administration of the realm. . . .

To Metz, then, let us direct our account, since we assembled there. Although the king found nothing there which belonged to him by right of domain, he nevertheless found all subject to him voluntarily, as had already been true at Verdun. And so, after camp had been pitched outside the city, he waited a few days for the army to arrive; and he enacted laws necessary for securing peace and other requirements on the journey, which the leaders confirmed by solemn oath. But because they did not observe them well, I have not preserved them either.

From Metz he sent ahead to Worms the prudent and pious men, Alvisus, bishop of Arras, and Leo, abbot of St. Bertin, to prepare for the army that followed a means of crossing the Rhine, which flowed past there; and they performed their task excellently, assembling from all sides a fleet so great that the army had no need for a bridge.

The people and the clergy of Worms received the king with the greatest festivity on the feast day of the Apostles Peter and Paul. Here we first perceived the foolish arrogance of our people. For the army crossed the Rhine, and, when they had found a broad expanse of meadow, the lord king decided to await the venerable Arnulf, bishop of Lisieux, and his Normans and English. From the city a great abundance of victuals came to us by river, and there was constant commerce between the natives and our people. Finally a quarrel arose; the pilgrims even threw the sailors into the river. Seeing this, the citizens of Worms rushed to arms, wounded several of our men, and killed one on the spot. The pilgrims were thrown into confusion by this crime; the poor clamored for fire, which was deadly both to certain of our men (rich merchants, that is, and money-changers) and to the citizens. By the will of God, however, wise men on both sides restrained the fools on both sides. Yet the citizens were still afraid; and, since they had removed the boats from both sides of the river, they halted the commerce. But that pious man, the bishop of Arras, after finding a boat with some difficulty, crossed the river with certain of the barons, calmed the crowd, and promised the citizens safety. Afterwards, when the boats had been brought back again, they engaged in commerce as before and furnished us with necessities. Hitherto, a foreboding about the people was entertained; here it was realized for the first time. Since everything was expensive because of the throng of people, many of the rank and file left us here and went through the Alps.

The king broke camp after he had sent the venerable bishop of

Arras and the chancellor and the abbot of St. Bertin ahead to Ratisbon to meet the emperor of Constantinople's messengers, who had been awaiting the king there for many days. At this city all crossed the Danube on a very fine bridge and found an ample fleet, which conveyed our baggage and many of the people as far as Bulgaria. Some even placed two- and four-horse carts on ship-board in order to compensate in the wastelands of Bulgaria for the losses which they had already endured, but both previously and afterward the carts afforded more hope than usefulness. We say all these things to caution subsequent pilgrims; for, since there was a very great number of four-horse carts, if one was damaged, all were delayed to the same extent; but, if they found many roads, all thronged them at the same time, and the packhorses, in avoiding the obstruction they presented, very frequently ran into more serious hindrances. For this reason the death of horses was a common occurrence, and so were the complaints about the short distance traveled each day.

The inhabitants of Ratisbon received the king in kingly style. But since I cannot repeat that phrase as often as the people showed him the devotion of their hearts, it should be said once and for all that all the towns, strongholds, and cities all the way to Constantinople showed him kingly honor, to a degree greater or less, yet all to the best of their ability. Now, although all were equally desirous of giving him a fine reception, I say "to a greater or less degree" because they did not all have the same resources.

Then, after camp had been pitched and the king provided with quarters, the emperor's messengers were summoned and came. When they had greeted the king and delivered their letters they stood to await his reply, for they would not sit unless commanded to do so; on command they arranged the chairs that they had brought with them and sat down. We saw there what we afterward learned is the Greek custom, namely, that the entire retinue remains standing while the lords are seated. One could see young men standing immobile, with heads bent and gaze directed intently and silently on their own lords, ready to obey their mere nod. They do not have cloaks, but the wealthy are clad in silken garments which are short, tight-sleeved, and sewn up on all sides, so that they always move about unimpeded, as do athletes. The poor outfit themselves in garments of like cut, but cheaper sort.

To interpret the documents fully is in part inappropriate, in part impossible, for me; for the first and greatest portion of them sought with such inept humility to secure our good will that I should say the words, too affectionate because they were not sprung from affection, were such as to disgrace not only an emperor, but even a buffoon. And therefore it is a shame for one to occupy himself with such matters when hurrying on to others. It is impossible for me, moreover, because French flatterers, even if they wish, cannot equal the Greeks. Now, although he blushed at it, the king at first allowed everything to be set forth; he did not know, however, from what source these compliments came. But finally, when messengers visited him repeatedly in Greece and always began with an introduction of this kind, he could scarcely endure it; and one time that pious and spirited man, Godfrey, bishop of Langres, taking pity on the king and not able to endure the delays caused by the speaker and interpreter, said, "Brothers, do not repeat 'glory,' 'majesty,' 'wisdom,' and 'piety' so often in reference to the king. He knows himself, and we know him well. Just indicate your wishes more briefly and freely." Nevertheless, the proverb "I fear the Greeks, even when they bear gifts" has always been well-known, even among certain laymen.

The last part of the letters, however, which was to the point, contained these two provisions: namely, that the king should not take any city or stronghold in the emperor's realm; that, on the contrary, if he drove the Turks from any place belonging to the emperor's domain, he should restore that place to the emperor; and this agreement was to be confirmed by oath on the part of the nobles. The first seemed very reasonable to our council; but in regard to the second the question about the emperor's domain was aired at length. Some said, "From the Turks he must try to acquire his domain either by purchase or negotiation or force; why should he not try to acquire it from us, too, if he should see us gain possession of it somehow?" Yet others said that his domain should be defined, so that a future quarrel could not be excited by the indefinite statement. Meanwhile, several days passed, and the Greeks protested against the delays, fearing, so they said, that the emperor would burn the food and destroy the fortifications by way of precaution. "For he warned us that he would do so if we delayed," they said, "on the ground of knowing from your delay that you were not coming peacefully. If he should do this, you would not thereafter find adequate supplies along your route, even though the emperor himself were willing that you should." At last, however, certain men swore to the security of the Greek realm on behalf of the king, and by a similar oath on behalf of their emperor the Greeks confirmed the promise of a sufficient market, suitable exchange, and other privileges which seemed necessary to us. The second provision, about which they could not come to a decision, they reserved, however, for a time when both sovereigns should be present. After these negotiations one of the Greeks, Demetrius by name, departed hastily; the other, who was called Maurus, stayed with us. Later the men were chosen who were to be sent ahead to Constantinople with this Maurus, whom I have mentioned (for the letters made this request among others)—Alvisus of Arras, Bartholomew the chancellor, Archibald of Bourbon, and certain others. Thus, when they had undertaken the embassy, they advanced swiftly, while the king followed slowly at the pace which the dense crowd would permit.

In this account the description of virtuous deeds furnishes the reader a good example, the names of towns indicate the route of the journey, the nature of the localities depicted suggests the caution which should be observed in provisioning. For never will there fail to be pilgrims to the Holy Sepulcher; and they will, I hope, be the more cautious because of our experiences. Well then—Metz, Worms, Würzburg, Ratisbon, and Passau, very wealthy towns, are each separated from the other by a three-day journey. From the last-named it is a five-day journey to Klosterneuburg: from there, one day's journey to the Hungarian border. The regions which lie between the towns are wooded, and if provisions should not be brought from the cities they cannot furnish an army with supplies. Nevertheless, they contain a wealth of streams, springs, and meadows. When I was crossing that territory I thought it rugged with mountains, but now, in comparison with Romania, I consider it level. On this side Hungary is bounded by muddy water; but on the other it is separated from Bulgaria by a clear stream. In its center flows the river Drave, of which one bank is sloping and the other steep, like a balk, with the result that the river overflows if a light rain falls and, when augmented by neighboring swamps, floods places which are even considerably distant. We heard that it had suddenly deluged many of the Germans who had preceded us, and we could hardly ford the place where their camp had been. For this crossing we had few ships and small, and so the horses had to swim. Since they entered the stream at an easy place and left it at a difficult one, they crossed with hardship indeed, but, by the aid of God, without loss. All the rest of the water in this land takes the form of lakes, swamps, and springs (if those are springs which travelers create, even in summer, by lightly digging the surface of the ground), with the exception of the Danube, which flows by in a fairly straight course and ships the wealth of many districts to the noted town of Gran. This land produces so much food that Julius Caesar's commissaries are said to have been located in it. Here we had such marketing privileges as we wished.

We took fifteen days to cross Hungary. Then, at the border, Bulgaria presented a fortified town called the Bulgarian Belgrad, to distinguish it from a Hungarian town of the same name, and thereafter, one day away and across a certain river, a poor little town, Brandiz. The rest of the country is wooded meadow or fodder-growing woodland, so to speak. It abounds in good things which grow of their own accord and would be suitable for other things if the region had cultivators. It is neither as flat-lying as a plain nor rugged with mountains, but is located among hills which are suitable for vines and grains, and it is watered by the very clearest springs and streams. It lacks rivers; for that matter, all the way from there to Constantinople we had no need of boats. On the fifth day's march the land reveals Nissa, the first (though small) city in this part of Greece. The cities Nissa, Sofia, Philippopolis, and Adrianople are a four-day journey one from another, and from Adrianople it is a five-day journey to Constantinople. The plains between the towns are full of villages, fortresses, and all kinds of resources. On the left and the right there are mountains, so near that you can see them and so far that a wide, rich, and pleasant plain is enclosed by them.

So much for these things! It is necessary to go back and forth—to progress and to turn back in my story—for although many things present themselves for description, the account should not be confused by the wealth of subjects. Many events happen at the same time, but in discourse one must observe a sequence. For instance, the king and the emperor both came to mind when I was writing about Ratisbon; for, although the king is my main subject, their mutual experiences force me to include a few words about the emperor. The German sovereign preceded ours in time and place: our king set out at Whitsuntide, the German king in the Easter season; our king departed from St. Denis, the German king from Ratisbon. The fact that the German king went first gave our king the advantage that, although there are many rivers in Germany, he found new bridges constructed over them without any expense or exertion on his part. Now, to tell the truth, the emperor set out in a most imperial fashion in respect to both fleet and land forces; this was advisable, for at that time the Hungarians were his enemies. Thus, the spirited emperor, who was both sailor and foot soldier (seeing that he had a very large army in the fleet with him and the horses and the rank and file beside him on the shore), entered Hungary as behooved and became a prince.

There was, moreover, a certain man named Boris who proclaimed a hereditary right to Hungary and who had sent letters to this effect to our king at Étampes, setting forth his complaint in full and humbly suing for justice. When coming to our king, following in the wake of his letters, he met the emperor, in whom he could trust. Therefore he set forth the case to him, promised him many things (indeed, as we have heard, gave him many things), and in turn received hope of gaining his right. But the king of Hungary, knowing that he could conquer more easily by gold than by force, poured out much money among the Germans and thus escaped an attack from them. Now Boris, who had been deluded by vain hope, hiding away as best he could, awaited the passage of our king and, with some strategem or other in mind, stealthily joined the Franks. It is said that two princes knew this, nevertheless, and that, because of the emperor of Constantinople whose niece he had married, Boris had joined the Franks with sufficient approbation on the part of those two. Protected and concealed by such shielding, he went through Hungary with the army.

Meanwhile the king of Hungary, fearing and revering our king, sought his favor by sending messengers and gifts, but he avoided crossing the Danube to meet him. He hoped for a conference with the man whom reputation had recommended to him (as the event showed), but, since he was afraid to cross to our side of the river, he humbly entreated the king to deign to come to his side. And so the king, whose wont it was to be won over easily by charity and humility, took along certain of his bishops and lords and gratified his wish. Then, after kisses, after embraces, they established a peace, strengthened their amity, and provided that from that time forth our pilgrims might pass through Hungary in safety. When he had accomplished this our king left the king of Hungary a happy man. Kingly gifts of horses, vases, and garments accompanied him, and the king of Hungary further intended to reverence our king, and his nobles insofar as he could, when, alas, he found out that Boris was with the Franks. He therefore sent men to propose a new treaty of friendship and peace with the king and to demand with humble supplication that his enemy, who was hiding in the army, be delivered to him. All this happened at night. However, the king, unacquainted with the extent of the duplicity, did not wholly believe the story; but at last he gave way to the messengers who were continually asserting it and beseeching his co-operation. Happy on this account, they proceeded more boldly than wisely; for Boris, roused from his bed by the noise made by those seeking him, escaped naked; and so they went away, their effort to no avail. Now, the fugitive was by no means stupid. When he had left the shelter of the tents, on the way to the river he encountered an esquire mounted on an excellent horse and struggled stoutly with him for the horse. The esquire cried out and resisted, and he prevailed more by his outcry than by his strength, for people appeared from every direction, and they seized Boris as if he were a robber and took him to the king, beaten, soiled with mud, and naked except for his breeches. Everyone thought he was a robber. But after he had thrown himself at the king's feet, even though he did not know our language and the king did not then have an interpreter, he, nevertheless, by mixing with his own language certain words we knew and by repeating his own name often, made known his identity. Presently, therefore, he was clad properly, and his case was reserved for the next day.

Now the Hungarian king, who had pitched his tents near us and who, as a result of his previous acquaintance with Boris, feared him, immediately found out what had happened, for he was close by and curious because of anxiety. He therefore demanded Boris from the king as from a friend and as if his surrender were obligatory according to their pact of amity; and in return he also made many promises which were hardly credible. Likewise, he stirred the minds of the nobles by his presence and presents; but neither the urgency of his supplications nor his gifts could obtain this request from the king before the council had rendered judgment. Our king said that the king of Hungary was his friend, but, nevertheless, that he must not do on behalf of the king anything which ill became a pilgrim. Then, when the bishops and the other magnates had been assembled and the matter had been examined, they decided that their king should preserve peace with the Hungarian king and that he should protect the life of the nobleman, even though he was a captive, because it would be a crime either to sell a man to death or, without cause, to break a treaty with a friend. Therefore the king of Hungary, not trusting himself to us, but departing with some distress, sought safety in a more remote part of his realm. Our king, however, keeping Boris with him, with due honor took him out of Hungary.

24. Anonymous Chronicler: Lisbon and Its Conquest by Crusaders

During these years Western Europe expanded into the Mediterranean area as well as along northern routes, as we know from the conquest of Syria and Palestine by the Crusades and of Moslem Sicily and Southern Italy by the Norman family of Guiscard. But the most dramatic advance was probably the effort, largely successful, to expel the Moslems from the Iberian peninsula, which we call the *Reconquista* or Reconquest. One episode in this *Reconquista* was the seizure of Lisbon from its Moslem rulers by a joint Portuguese-North European crusading force during the course of the Second Crusade. A portion of the tale of this conquest by an unknown chronicler is related here. It gives one an excellent description of Moslem Spain during these years and how non-Spanish Christian forces often behaved after they had captured a Moslem city—which explains why Moslem resistance to Crusaders increased during the course of the twelfth century. Finally, one should note that the crusading forces who took Lisbon contained few nobles, but were mainly composed of humble German, English, and Flemish merchants who probably made up most of the crusading armies at this time. [From *The Conquest of Lisbon,* ed. and trans. Charles W. David (New York: Columbia University Press, 1936), pp. 89–97 and 173–81. Copyright 1936 by Columbia University Press. Reprinted with the omission of footnotes by permission of the publisher.]

When we had passed the night on the aforesaid island, we set sail at dawn and had a prosperous voyage until, when we were almost at the mouth of the Tagus River, a squall came down from the hills of Cintra and struck the ships with such amazing violence that several of the smaller boats were sunk with the men on board. And the squall continued until we entered the shelter of the Tagus River. As we were entering the port a wonderful portent appeared to us in the air. For behold, great white clouds coming along with us from the direction of the Gauls were seen to encounter other great clouds bespattered with blackness coming from the mainland. Like ordered lines of battle with left wings locked together they collided with a marvelous impact, some in the manner of skirmishers attacking on right and left and then springing back into line, some encircling others in order to find a way through, some going right through the others and reducing them to a void like vapor, some being pressed downwards and now almost touching the water, others being lifted upwards and now borne from view in the firmament. When at last the great cloud coming from our direction and carrying with it all the impurity of the air, so that all on this side appeared as purest azure, pressed back all the others which were coming from the direction of the mainland, and, as a victress driving the booty before her, held all alone the mastery of the air, and all the others had either been reduced to nothing, or, if some fragments remained, they appeared to be in flight towards the city, we all shouted, "Behold, our cloud has conquered! Behold, God is with us! The power of our enemies is destroyed! They are confounded, for the Lord has put them to flight!" And so at last the squall ceased. And a short time afterwards, about the tenth hour of the day, we arrived at the city which is not far from the mouth of the Tagus.

The Tagus, gliding by, is a river which flows down from the region of Toledo. Gold is found on its banks in the early spring after it has returned to its channel. It contains fish in such quantities that it is believed by the natives to be two parts water and one part fish; and it abounds in shellfish like the sands [without number]. This also is especially to be noted, that the fish in this river retain at all seasons their richness and natural flavor, neither altering nor deteriorating, as happens with you, under any circumstances. To the south of it lies the province of Almada, which abounds in vines and figs and pomegranates. So fertile is the soil that two crops are produced from a single seeding. It is celebrated for its hunting and abounds in honey. Also on this side is the castle of Palmela. On the north of the Tagus is the city of Lisbon, situated on the top of a round hill; and its walls, descending by degrees, extend right down to the bank of the river, which is only shut out by the wall. At the time of our arrival [it was] the richest in trade of all Africa and a good part of Europe. It is situated on *Mons Artabrum,* a promontory which extends to the Ocean of Cadiz [and forms a landmark], dividing the land, the sea, and the heavens; for the side of Spain ends there, and with the rounding of the promontory its northern front and the Gallic Ocean begin, the Atlantic and the West having there been terminated. It is the site where the town of Lisbon is believed to have been founded by Ulysses. The surrounding country is second to none and comparable with the best, rich in products of the soil, whether you are looking for the fruit of trees or of vines. It abounds in everything, both costly articles of luxury and necessary articles of consumption. It also contains gold and silver and is never wanting in iron mines. The olive flourishes. There is nothing unproductive or sterile or which refuses to return a harvest. They do not boil their salt but dig it. Figs are so abundant that we could hardly eat a fraction of them. Even the dry places are productive of forage. The region is celebrated for many kinds of hunting. There are no hares, but many kinds of birds. The air is healthful, and the city has hot baths. About eight miles away is the castle of Cintra, in which there is a spring of purest water, the use of which is said to stop coughs and allay consumption. Hence, if the inhabitants should hear anyone coughing, they might discern that he was not a native. The region also produces citrons. In its pastures the mares breed with a wonderful fecundity; for, being blown upon by the west winds, they conceive from the wind, and afterwards, being in heat, they are joined with their mates, and so they are impregnated by the breath of the breezes.

At the time of our arrival the city consisted of sixty thousand families paying taxes, if you include the adjacent suburbs, with the exception of the free ones which are subject to the exactions of no one. The hilltop is girdled by a circular wall, and the walls of the city extend downward on the right and left to the bank of the Tagus. And the suburbs which slope down beneath the wall have been so cut out of the rocks that each of the steep defiles which they have in place of ordinary streets may be considered a very well fortified stronghold, with such obstacles is it girt about. The city was populous beyond what can readily be believed; for, as after its capture we learned from their alcayde, that is, their governor, it contained one hundred and fifty-four thousand men, without counting women and children, but including the citizens of Santarém, who had this year been expelled from their castle and were sojourning in the city as newcomers, and all the aristocracy of Cintra and Almada and Palmela, and many merchants from all parts of Spain and Africa. But although they were so numerous, they had equipment in lances and shields for but fifteen thousand; and with these they went out by turns as the proclamation of the governor had determined. The buildings of the city were so closely packed together that, except in the merchants' quarter, hardly a street could be found which was more than eight feet wide. The cause of so great a population was that there was no prescribed form of religion among them, for everyone was a law unto himself; for the most depraved elements from all parts of the world had flowed together as it were into a cesspool and had formed a breeding ground of every lust and abomination. In the time of the Christian kings, before the Moors took it, the memory of three martyrs was celebrated beside the city in a place called Campolide, namely, the martyrs Verissimus and Maxima and Julia the Virgin, whose church, though razed to the ground by the Moors, still reveals, in sign of its ruin, just three stones which it has never been possible to carry away; concerning which, some say they may have altars, but others gravestones. Let this suffice for the present concerning the city.

*   *   *

[Some weeks later after the siege had dragged on] when all had returned to camp, they decided that an attempt should be made to enter the city at the point of the sword. Meanwhile, the men of Cologne and the Flemings, waxing indignant because the king, as it seemed, was favoring the hostages, rushed out of their camps under arms in order that they might seize the hostages with violence from the king's camp and take vengeance upon them. And there was tumult and clashing of arms all around. But since we were still engaged in conversation and awaiting the turn of events in the middle ground between the king's camp and theirs, we reported to the king what was about to happen. But when Christian, leader of the Flemings, and the count of Aerschot learned of the outbreak of their forces, they promptly put a stop to it, although they were hardly armed. Then, when the tumult had been quieted, they went to conciliate the king on behalf of their forces, protesting that they themselves were innocent of this action. Accordingly, when he had taken security from them and had at last recovered his temper, he ordered that their forces should put away their arms, declaring roundly that he would postpone the siege until the morrow; and he said that he would not put honor second even to the taking of the city, that, on the contrary, he would account all things for naught if it should be wanting; indeed, that disgraced by these outrages, he was unwilling any longer to associate with abandoned men—the most insolent desperadoes who would do anything. Finally, having with difficulty recovered his equanimity, he agreed to consider what he wished to be done upon the morrow. And so it was decided next day that our leaders from both divisions for themselves and for their men should swear fealty to the king, to be kept so long as they remained in his country.

When these matters had thus been settled on both sides, the terms of the surrender of the city on which the Moors had insisted on the previous day were conceded. Acccordingly, it was decided among ourselves that one hundred and forty armed men from our forces and one hundred and sixty from the men of Cologne and the Flemings should enter the city before all the others, and without violence occupy the stronghold of the upper castle, in order that within the same the enemy might bring their money and possessions, acknowledged under oath, before our men, and that, after these things had all been collected, the city might be searched by our forces—if anything more should be found in anybody's possession, the owner of the house in which it should be discovered was to be made to suffer for it with his head—and that in this manner the whole population, after it had been despoiled, should be released outside the walls. And so, the gate having been opened and an opportunity of entering obtained for those who had been chosen for the purpose, the men of Cologne and the Flemings, contriving deception by a clever argument, obtained the consent of our men that they should go in first for the sake of their honor. And when they had thus obtained permission and an opportunity of entering first, more than two hundred of them slipped in along with those who had been designated, as above mentioned, besides others whom they had already introduced through the breach in the wall which stood open on their side. But none of our forces presumed to enter, except those who had been designated. And so, the archbishop and his fellow bishops leading the way with a banner bearing the sign of the cross, our leaders, together with the king and those who had been chosen for the purpose, made their entry.

Oh, what rejoicing there was on the part of all! Oh, what especial pride on the part of all! Oh, what a flow of tears of joy and piety, when, to the praise and honor of God and of the most holy Virgin Mary, the ensign of the salvation-bearing cross was beheld by all placed upon the highest tower in token of the subjection of the city, while the archbishop and the bishops together with the clergy and all the people, not without tears, intoned with a wonderful jubilation the *Te Deum laudamus* together with the *Asperges me* and devout prayers! The king, meanwhile, made the circuit of the walls of the upper castle on foot.

Thereupon the men of Cologne and the Flemings, when they

saw so many temptations to greed in the city, observed not the bond of their oath or plighted faith. They rushed about hither and thither; they pillaged; they broke open doors; they tore open the innermost parts of every house; they drove out the citizens and treated them with insults, against right and justice; they scattered utensils and clothing; they insulted maidens; they made wrong equal with right; they secretly snatched away all those things which ought to have been made the common property of all the forces. They even slew the aged bishop of the city, against all right and decency, by cutting his throat. They seized the alcayde himself and carried everything out of his house. And his mare (above mentioned), the count of Aerschot seized with his own hands, and at the demand of the king and of all our men that he give her up, he held on to her so obstinately that, because with an emission of blood she had lost her foal, the alcayde himself spoke out and branded the abominable action as disgusting. But the Normans and the English, for whom good faith and scruples of conscience were matters of the highest import, remained quietly at the posts to which they had been assigned, while they wondered what such an event might portend, preferring to keep their hands from all rapine rather than violate their engagements and the ordinances of the oath-bound association—an episode which covered the count of Aerschot and Christian and their principal followers with shame, since through the disregarding of their oath their un-mixed greed now stood openly revealed to us. But finally having come to their senses, they obtained from us by insistent prayers that our men upon the same footing with theirs should peacefully bring together the remainder of the booty of the city with the portions already collected, in order that thus at last after shares had been apportioned to all, they might nullify the insults and the thefts in peace by being prepared to give satisfaction for what they had wrongfully taken in advance.

Accordingly, when the enemy within the city had been despoiled, from early Saturday morning until the following Wednesday so great a multitude of people was seen steadily filing out through three gates that it seemed as if all Spain had flowed together into it. Then we learned of a very wonderful miracle, namely, that for a fortnight before the capture of the city the victuals of the enemy became inedible on account of an intolerable stench, al-though afterwards they tasted agreeable and acceptable both to us and to them. And when the city had been ransacked, we found in the cellars as much as eight thousand seams of wheat and barley, and twelve thousand sextars of oil. Concerning their religion. . . . in their temple, which rises aloft on seven rows of columns surmounted by as many arches, we found almost two hundred corpses, besides more than eight hundred sick persons who were staying there in all their filth and squalor.

When the city had been taken after we had besieged it for seventeen weeks, the inhabitants of Cintra surrendered the stronghold of their castle and gave themselves up to the king. And the castle of Palmela, after it had been evacuated by its garrison, was occupied by the king while empty. And so, the strongholds appurtenant to the city in the surrounding country having been taken, the name of the Franks was magnified throughout all parts of Spain, and terror seized upon the Moors among whom tidings of this action were made known.

Then Gilbert of Hastings was chosen from among our forces to be bishop, and the king, the archbishop, his fellow bishops, the clergy, and the laity all gave their assent to his election. And on the day on which the memory of All Saints is celebrated, to the glory and honor of the name of Christ and of his most holy Mother, the temple was purified by the archbishop and his four fellow bishops, and the episcopal see was restored therein, with jurisdiction over the following castles and villages: beyond Tagus, the castle of Alcácer do Sal, the castle of Palmela, the province of Almada; on this side of Tagus, the castle of Cintra, the castle of Santarém, the castle of Leiria. And its limits extend from Alcácer to Leiria, and from the western sea to the city of Évora.

Then there followed such a pestilence among the Moors that throughout the desert wastes, in vineyards, in villages, and squares, and among ruins of houses unnumbered thousands of corpses lay exposed to birds and beasts; and living men resembling bloodless beings went about the earth, and, grasping the symbol of the cross, they kissed it as suppliants and declared that Mary the Mother of God was good, so that in all their acts and speeches, even when already *in extremis,* they interspersed the words *Maria bona, bona Maria,* and cried out pitiably.

25. Three Chroniclers: Richard the Lionhearted's Capture in Austria

Richard the Lionhearted (1189–1199) was the worst ruler and the most talented general among England's medieval kings. He was also very much a hero during his own lifetime, probably because of his skill in battle and his knightly habit of largesse, which made him an outstanding example of the use of conspicuous consumption. Thus his capture in Vienna by the Duke of Austria on his way back from the Holy Land and his subsequent incarceration by the Emperor Henry VI caused quite a stir in Europe until a huge ransom was paid. The three chroniclers whose accounts of this affair are given here, Matthew Paris, Ralph of Coggeshall, and an anonymous chronicler called Ernoul, all present different facets of this story and help explain Richard's positive genius for making enemies. They are also of interest because they show us how precarious sea travel was during this period and help to remind us that during the twelfth and thirteenth centuries the possession of ample supplies of money was a major key to military and political success. [From *The Crusade of Richard I, 1189–92* by T. A. Archer (London: Long Acre, 1900), pp. 334–43. Reprinted by permission of The Hamlyn Publishing Group Limited.]

Matthew Paris: The Causes of the Duke of Austria's Enmity Against Richard

About this time [c. June 1192] came the Duke of Austria to Acre. . . . And when his marshals, going ahead, had made choice of a resting-place and prepared the things that were necessary for him, there came up precipitately a certain knight belonging to king Richard's train, a Norman by race. Now this man, who, after the manner of his trible, was over-brimming with pride, declared that he had a better right to this abode than any one else. For to him and his comrades he declared it had been assigned on their first arrival.

And there was much quarrelling, till the din of it reached the king's ears. Now he, being over-well disposed to the cause of the Norman, waxed wroth with the duke's train and forgetting the God-like moderation of "I will go down and see," gave a headstrong, unseemly order for the duke's banner to be cast into a cesspool.

And when the duke knew of this and how that he had been deprived of his abode and basely insulted by Norman jesters, he brought his grievance before the king, from whom however he could get no justice. Whereupon, being scorned by an earthly king, he turned him to the King of Kings and invoked the Lord God to whom vengeance belongs. And soon after he hastened home being shamed and in confusion; and there was no little shame to king Richard by reason of this thing later on.

Ralph of Coggeshall: King Richard's Shipwreck and Capture

Whilst the king Richard, after this incredible victory, was staying for six weeks at Joppa, a certain baleful disease born of the air's corruption settled upon him and almost all his men to their great damage; for, with the exception of the king, to whom the Lord granted a safe recovery, as many as were stricken with the illness died off quickly. Then king Richard, seeing that his treasure which he had been distributing to his knights with too liberal a hand was beginning to fail; seeing, too, that the army of the French and other strangers whom he had hired and kept with him for a year at his own expense wished to go home; seeing that his own army was gradually growing less, owing partly to engagements with the enemy and partly to the baleful sickness, whilst the number of his foes increased every day, took counsel of the brethren of the Temple and the Hospital, as well as of the leaders who were with him. He was minded to go home at once with the intention of returning with greater store of knights and treasure. To this he pledged himself with an oath, giving security also. And there was an additional reason in the news as to how his brother, earl John, whom he had left in England, was plotting to subdue that country, and had already deposed his chancellor on the pretext of tyranny.

So in the autumn, when his ships were ready and his affairs all

duly arranged, king Richard, the lady, queen Berengaria, his sister
Joan, queen of Sicily, and his nobles, together with the army, crossed
the Mediterranean. As they were setting off by the just judgment of
God there sprung up unusual tempests. Some suffered shipwreck,
and barely got to shore with the loss of all their wealth after their
ships had been battered to pieces; but a few reached their intended
harbour in safety. Those who escaped the perils of the sea found
hostile ranks rise up against them everywhere on shore. They were
pitilessly taken prisoner, robbed, and soon burdened with a heavy
ransom. They had no place of safety left, just as if land and sea had
banded together against the fugitives of God. Whence it was sufficiently clear that God was wrath at their return before completing
their pilgrimage. For he had intended to magnify them greatly in
that land, after a short season [of trial], by subduing all their
enemies and handing over to them the land on whose behalf they
had undertaken so toilsome a pilgrimage. For in the very Lent after
their departure the enemy of the Christian faith, the invader of the
land in question, to wit Saladin, ended his life by a miserable death.
Now had they been present at that time they might easily have
seized the whole land, seeing that the sons and kinsmen of Saladin
began to quarrel among themselves.

But king Richard, after being tempest-tossed with some of his
comrades for six weeks (during which time sailing towards Barbary,
he had come within three days of Marseilles), learnt by frequent
reports that the count of St. Giles and all the princes through whose
lands he was about to pass had banded together against him, and
were laying snares for him everywhere. Accordingly he made up
his mind to go home secretly by way of Dutchland [Germany] and,
turning his sails, at last reached the island of Corfu. There he hired
two beaked pirate-vessels. For you must know the pirates had dared
to attack the king's ship but, on being recognised by one of the
sailors, had entered into a league with [Richard]. The king, knowing their bravery and boldness, went on board with these pirates,
taking with him also Baldwin de Betun, master Philip, the king's
clerk, and Anselm, the chaplain, who brought us word of all these
things as he saw and heard them.

Certain brothers of the Temple also went with him, and they
all landed on the coast of Sclavonia near a certain town called
Gazara [Ragusa], from which place they at once sent a messenger
to the nearest castle begging a safe conduct from its lord, who
chanced to be the marquis's nephew. Now, on his return, the king
had brought three precious stones, to wit three rubies, from a certain

Pisan, to whom he paid 900 besants for them. One of these while on board he had set in a gold ring, and this ring he sent to the lord of the castle by the aforesaid messenger. This messenger, when asked by the castle-lord for whom he was seeking a safe conduct, made answer that it was for pilgrims returning from Jerusalem. Thereupon the lord asked for their names, to which the messenger replied: "One of them is called Baldwin de Betun; but the other, who has sent you this ring, is called Hugh the merchant." Then that lord, having regarded the ring for a long while, rejoined: "Nay, he is not called Hugh but king Richard," adding, "though I have sworn to take prisoner all the pilgrims coming from those parts, and to receive no gift at their hands, yet by reason of the noble gift and the lord who sends it as a gift of honour to me whom he does not know, I will return him his gift and give him free leave to depart."

So the messenger, returning, brought back this news to the king, who, with his comrades, trembling greatly, got their horses ready in the mid of night, stealthily quitted the town and, in this fashion, set out through the land. For some time they proceeded without molestation. But the lord we have spoken of before sent out a spy to his brother, bidding him seize the king when he reached his territory. When the king had entered the city where this lord's brother dwelt, the latter called in a very faithful follower, Roger de Argenton, a Norman by birth. Now, to this man, who had dwelt with him for twenty years and married his niece, he gave orders to take special note of the houses where pilgrims were in the habit of lodging and to see, if by any chance, he could discover the king through his speech or any other sign. This lord made his follower promise of half his city if he could intercept the king. So this Roger, routing and enquiring at every inn, at last found the king, who, after long attempts at hiding his personality, in the end yielded to the earnest prayers and tears of his dutiful questioner and confessed what rank he held. Upon this Roger, anxious for his safety, gave him a very goodly steed, begging him take to flight and without any delay. After this, returning to his own lord, Roger said that the talk about the king's coming was an idle rumour. [The strangers, he added,] were Baldwin de Betun and his comrades, who were on their way back from their pilgrimage; upon which the lord, mad with rage, gave orders for all to be arrested.

Meanwhile, the king, leaving the city stealthily, in the company of William de Stagno and a certain lad, who could speak German, journeyed three days and nights without food. Then, being hard pressed by hunger, he turned aside to a certain town called Vienna near the Danube in Austria, a place where—to put the finishing stroke to all his woes—the duke of Austria was then staying. Thither the king's boy came to make a purchase; and, as he offered more besants than he should have done and comported himself with overmuch state and pomp, he was seized upon by the citizens. On being asked who he was he made answer that he was the servant of a very rich merchant, who would reach that city in three days. Then, being set free, he returned secretly to the king's retreat, telling the king all that had happened and urging him to flee at once. But the king, after his great hardships at sea, was eager to rest a few days in this city. Now when this lad went [more often than was safe] to the public market, he chanced once on the day of St. Thomas the Apostle imprudently to carry his lord the king's gloves under his belt. The magistrates of the city, learning this, seized the boy a second time and, after many and fearful tortures, threatened to cut out his tongue unless he confessed the truth quickly; till he, constrained by torments he could not bear, told them how things really stood. Whereupon the magistrates, after carrying the news to the duke, surrounded the king's retreat and demanded that he should yield of his own accord.

Ernoul: How King Richard Was Taken Captive

When [king Richard] had made truce with the Saracens he had his ships and his galleys fitted out and laden with provisions and people. Then he put on board his wife and his sister and the emperor of Cyprus' wife (the emperor himself had died in prison) the emperor's daughter, his knights, and his sergeants. Then came he to the Master of the Temple and said: "Sir, I know well that all folks do not love me, and I know well that, if I cross the sea in such a manner as to be recognised, I shall reach no place where I shall not be liable to death or captivity. Now I pray you, for the love of God, that you give me certain of your knights and your serving-brothers to accompany me in a galley, and after we have reached land to conduct me in peace to my own country as though I were a Templar."

The Master said that he would willingly do so. Then secretly he got knights and sergeants ready and made them go on board a galley; after which the king, taking leave of count Henry, the Templars, and the men of the land, [at] even entered the galley where the Templars were. He also bade farewell to his wife and his own train; the one party going one way and the other another. But the king of England could not do things so secretly as to escape detection; or as to prevent [an enemy] entering the galley with him to secure his apprehension. And [this enemy] went with him till he landed and further yet. . . .

When the Templars and the king of England had arrived [at Aquilea] they purchased sufficient conveyances, and mounting them proceeded by way of Germany. And he who had got abroad to secure the king's apprehension was with them still. And he accompanied them till they rested in one of the Duke of Austria's castles in Germany. And it chanced that the Duke of Austria was then at the castle.

Now, when he who was pursuing the king knew that the Duke was in the castle, he came to him and said: "Sir, now is the chance of doing yourself a good turn. The king of England is lodged in this town: take heed that he does not escape." The Duke was greatly delighted at hearing this news, for some folk say that the king had done him shame in the army before Acre. Accordingly he bade his people close the castle gates; and putting on his own arms made his men don theirs and went to the inn where (the king) was resting, taking with him the man who had brought the news that he might identify the king.

Now it was told the king of England how they were coming to the house to seize him; and in his surprise he knew not what to do. Wherefore he took a mean jacket and threw it over his back to disguise himself and so entered the kitchen, and sat down to turn the capons at the fire.

Then the Duke's men entered the house and made search here and there, but only found the Temple folk and those who were attending to the food in the kitchen. Then he who had betrayed the king entered the kitchen and saw the king turning the capons as we have said. Then he went up to him and said to him, "Master, get up; too long hast thou tarried there already." Then he said to the duke's knights, "Sirs, behold him here and take him." And they laid hands on him and took him and put him in prison.

SOURCES OF CIVILIZATION IN THE WEST

Robert Lee Wolff, *General Editor*

OTHER BOOKS IN THE SERIES